AN ETHIOPIAN FAMILY'S JOURNEY OF ENTREPRENEURSHIP IN THE US

Yoni Medhin

AN ETHIOPIAN FAMILY'S JOURNEY OF ENTREPRENEURSHIP IN THE US

A Story of Determination, Resourcefulness, and Faith

The Emergent Entrepreneur Collection

Collection Editor
Drew Harris

LPp

First published in 2024 by Lived Places Publishing

British Library Cataloguing in Publication Data
A CIP record for this book is available from the British Library

ISBN: 9781915734266 (pbk)
ISBN: 9781915734280 (ePDF)
ISBN: 9781915734273 (ePUB)

Cover design by Fiachra McCarthy
Book design by Rachel Trolove of Twin Trail Design
Typeset by Newgen Publishing UK

Lived Places Publishing
Long Island
New York 11789

www.livedplacespublishing.com

Abstract

This memoir chronicles Yonatan Medhin's entrepreneurial journey in founding Grain4Grain, a startup aiming to upcycle brewery byproducts into sustainable ingredients. It begins with Yonatan's family background as Ethiopian immigrants and follows their journey in the US and his entrepreneurial journey. He details securing initial funding, many pitches, partnering with customers, the impact of Covid-19, scaling production, and ultimately the failure and wind-up of the business. Throughout the ups and downs, Yonatan reflects on mistakes made and lessons learned about financials, business systems, investors, customers, and many other themes and points. He concludes with encouragement for future entrepreneurs to pursue their passions despite the inevitable challenges of building a business.

Keywords

Sustainable business; immigration; community; identity; lived experience; trauma; success; challenges; inspiration; real estate

Acknowledgments

I want to thank my Dad, Mom, Bethel, Nati, and Jen. Dad and Mom, you two are special people and the world has become a better place because of you two and your dedication to us and God. Love you all.

Contents

Learning objectives

1. Analyze the key strategic decisions and pivotal moments that impacted the trajectory of Grain4Grain.
2. Evaluate the leadership, management, and personal qualities exhibited by Yoni throughout his entrepreneurial journey.
3. Examine the process of developing and scaling a novel production technology and bringing it to market.
4. Assess the viability of sustainable/upcycling ventures and strategies for overcoming barriers to adoption.
5. Synthesize lessons learned from Yoni's entrepreneurial failures and successes applicable to business and leadership roles.
6. Examine the challenges and opportunities Yoni's parents faced as Ethiopian immigrants building a life in the United States.
7. Analyze the strategies and investments Yoni's parents used to accumulate assets and build wealth over time.
8. Evaluate the role of faith, community, and values in shaping Yoni's family's business ventures and approach to entrepreneurship.
9. Assess how Yoni's parents' entrepreneurial example influenced his ambitions and mindset as a founder.
10. Synthesize lessons from Yoni's family's journey about opportunity, sacrifice, risk-taking, and creating value as immigrants and entrepreneurs.

1
Why am I doing this?

How Grain4Grain almost collapsed because of Covid—fall 2020 to winter 2020

As of now, I have probably met over 100 entrepreneurs, and the age-old adage that you will face challenges that will test your deepest resolve to continue forward has never been truer during my tenure as CEO of Grain4Grain. I co-founded Grain4Grain in the summer of 2018 with the vision of making sustainable ingredients affordable and accessible for everyone. For me, along with the rest of the world, Covid-19 was a glaring exposé for Grain4Grain. It exposed everything we knew with greater perception and clarity, and it also exposed things we did not know. Before Covid-19, I thought I knew what I was doing. I was highly focused on growing our consumer packaged goods (CPG) brand, networking for our seed fundraising round, and hiring at our facility to help offload manufacturing duties. However, Covid-19 exposed realities that I wish were untrue. Here is a list of just a few of my realizations during the summer of 2020:

- Having many deficiencies, ranging from a poor management skill set (which has improved) to a classic case of people-pleasing, has inevitably caused numerous issues.

- Trying to start a food technology manufacturing firm with only $160,000 of starting capital is really, really hard.

- Working with a co-founder who is part time and has already expressed the desire to quit is not the most brilliant idea.

- Having a board that is only interested when things are going well or when things are going bad can be incredibly isolating.

- And many, many more.

As the summer continued, my co-founder inevitably did use the opportunity to leave and pursue another career pathway, and the ensuing difficulty of supply chain constraints plus lack of financing crippled the CPG business. For example, due to the difficulties of maintaining a presence on shelves, many flocked to online channels. However, when everyone is suddenly rushing to a channel not optimized for that level of traffic, prices increase. And boy, did they increase a lot. Suddenly, advertisement costs increased by nearly four to five times. So, as with any business that is barreling toward bankruptcy, you pause your advertisement spend, and voila, almost all the revenue is gone. Grain4Grain went almost two months with nearly $0 coming in. So, let's rewind to the late summer of 2020 when I was walking in the dog park, contemplating winding the business down. I quickly thought through a few reasons why. For months, Grain4Grain had been operating on a razor-thin margin of working capital. Strategic decision-making had been simply due to immediate necessity rather than strategizing for potential long-term payoffs.

Finally, Grain4Grain hac been facing the impending day when our last remaining a nount of cash would run out.

Fateful phone calls

At the dog park, I worked through the quick math of what Grain4Grain's outstanding liabilities included and determined the priorities for what needed to be paid before we attempted to liquidate our equipment. As I wrapped up the somewhat futile attempt to reconcile the books with my phone calculator, I received the first of two somewhat life-changing calls. The first call was from an organization called LiftFund. LiftFund is an organization that exists to help small businesses attain more traditional financing (traditional for the sake of this book = interest-bearing financing; think bank loans) through local and federal mechanisms that are there to encourage entrepreneurship and small business growth. About six months prior, when Grain4Grain was getting our products onto shelves, we had the opportunity to take out a loan with LiftFund at a very favorable rate. Several examples of financial assistance available through LiftFund include, but are not limited to, 0 per cent interest loans (artificially depressed through funding from the city or county), Small Business Administration (SBA) loans (loans that are partially or majorly guaranteed by the federal government), and loan forgiveness via eliminating the note altogether, in effect turning it into a grant.

Before diving into the call with LiftFund, it is important to understand the financing options available throughout the Covid-19 pandemic. During the pandemic, there was a wave of stimulus from the Federal Reserve and our lawmakers to help aid companies during the lockdowns. These included the Paycheck Protection Program, better known as the PPP loan, and the Disaster Relief Fund. Through these two mechanisms, thousands and thousands of businesses that had their landscape change for them overnight (whether through immense disruption or outright shutdown) were able to request funding. Yet this funding had very finicky standards of distribution. For example, the PPP loan generally operated like this: Company A, which had 100 employees and was forced to shut down during the initial and subsequent outbreaks, was allowed to request funding through their bank. Their bank would then check their request and disperse enough money to cover the paychecks of Company A's employees. For Grain4Grain, however, our employees were considered independent contractors, due to the nature of our work, and unfortunately we found out that this disqualified us from applying to any PPP loans during the pandemic. The second option of relief, and the more variable of the two, was the Disaster Relief Loan. This, like the PPP loan, was a stimulus given to banks and lenders that were tasked with helping the businesses that banked or worked with them in some sort of capacity. About six months prior, we had the opportunity to take out a loan with LiftFund when we were getting onto shelves with our first products at a very favorable rate at the time. Now LiftFund was also offering payment delays to many of the notes they had issues with during Covid-19, including ours. Keep in mind, this was very common at the time, and was also a tactic deployed by commercial landlords, including ours, knowing that businesses that operated physical locations could and mostly were severely impacted by the pandemic. While that loan had payments that were delayed, our first payment was approaching.

In fact, it was two days from when I was at the dog park that day in late summer 2020. But the call I received from LiftFund was not anything I expected. The very kind woman over the phone began to describe that, through an "internal determination" by their underwriters and loan officers, coupled with the availability of funds through the various Disaster Relief Funds that were issued in San Antonio, Texas, and federally, Grain4Grain would be granted full forgiveness for our loan. In essence, this converted our loan from a liability to grant income. The phone call concluded with me saying thank you, going back to my "what we owe" tab, and deleting the now forgiven loan. Essentially, what I was thinking is that, if we decided to stop Grain4Grain, we would owe nothing, and would have equipment that we could liquidate and walk away unscathed. I had been doing this for almost two years with relatively good press and good overall progress that I was pretty proud of. When it became clear that we were potentially closing our doors, I started using a vague metric called "what pops up when you google me or the business", and by having more positive and real results, I felt the chance of me getting into a higher-caliber MBA program or a coveted job at a leading company after closing down Grain4Grain.

While still at the dog park, I received the second of the fateful calls that would change the course of my life. A newly made friend from the startup community reached out and asked me if I would be interested in entering a pitch competition. If there is one thing I do well, it is my uncanny ability to convince and command an audience from a stage. So, I was intrigued. He proceeded to describe a "tech" competition known as TechFuel. The city of San Antonio and the influential Bexar (pronounced "bear") County, desperate in its attempts to attract budding tech entrepreneurs from the alluring, startup ecosystem of its not-so-far-away neighbor Austin, earmarked funds to be utilized as a grant to be given in a competition. The amount being given out was significant when compared to previous grants, with the top prize being $50,000. I was intrigued with the pitch competition, but also skeptical. Until this point, I had not thought of Grain4Grain as "tech", or at least not in terms of the established understanding of digital and information technology. Sure, we operated a unique manufacturing technology (which I will share more about in Chapter 3), but we did not develop any new types of software or applications. I had some ideas for that, but I was barely affording our dumpster company, so these were pipedreams at best. What my friend encouraged me to do was to reframe Grain4Grain as a company utilizing proprietary technology to enable a brand-new process and ingredient into the market—rather than the more traditional CPG food business we normally described ourselves as. And that was it. Grain4Grain's greatest strength was not the brand, the recipes for our products, or the personalities that operated the business. Our greatest strength was the fact that we could turn almost any byproduct into a food-safe ingredient with a process that had already gone through the scrutiny of food safety regulators and professionals. That has tremendous value, and at the heart of that value was our technology driving the vision of making sustainable ingredients affordable and available. He said there would be an initial "quarter-finals pitch" that he would get me a spot for, then after that, it was up to me and my people-coaxing skills to take us further. "Remember, you are tech", he said as he hung up.

As I concluded my alarmingly disorienting morning at the dog park, I made some calls to a mentor and (now former) co-founder to discuss the conversations we had. As I arrived home, I immediately dug up all of Grain4Grain's pitch decks and began the dredging and beer-filled nights of redoing what I had spent so much time last year making. The TechFuel competition had some difficult constraints (that I can now appreciate). The first constraint was that the pitch could not exceed three minutes. Within a total of five minutes, introductions, the pitch, and Q&A must be completed. Well, sadly, our most recent deck was very long relative to the standards for the competition since it had been used for a potential investment offer and an application to an accelerator. As I began to trim the presentation, I found myself struggling to find the main and simplified point (a deficiency that I continue to improve upon). But the beer helped. I was able to trim it down to what amounted to a deck that required me to speed talk through major points of our story, margins, vision, and team.

Pitch night

The setup for the quarter-finals of the TechFuel competition was simple enough. The city had gathered a litany of businesses to send in, via Zoom of course, to a virtual pitch hall, where the various entrepreneurs would enter competing pools and compete for the top two slots per pool. Now, keep in mind, most of the businesses barely existed or were still in the ideation phase. We had actual paying customers, a fledgling retail presence of close to 200 stores, and some future potential to expand, given we had the funding. So, the quarter-finals presentation came and went a couple of weeks after that first phone call, and we found out fairly quickly that we would be heading to the finals. For several reasons, it was clear that our pitch, while good enough to make it through the quarter-finals of the competition, would be inadequate to make it through the finals stage. Our primary audience was changing from professionals in various fields to the general public across a variety of social media platforms. This new audience, I figured, was less interested in the facts of our technology, the advantageous margins it created in the market, or the various specifications that made us more efficient than our competitors. They wanted a story. Everyone wants a story. A tangible start, an exciting journey, with the conclusion being a triumphal end. The setup for the finals would be that there was a panel of judges, similar to the judges we had during the quarter-finals, with comparable backgrounds and professions— however, the main difference was that these judges carried no weight in their votes. There would be an audience that would tune in during the competition, and at the conclusion of every three-minute pitch, there was a two-minute Q&A with the judges, followed by a two-minute voting period online. The audience tuning in online were the ones carrying out the vote and deciding the winner.

Because of how fast the pitch and Q&A would be, we needed to transition our pitch into a quick story that would help explain the business and value prop to folks that presumably had no background in food or food technology. I engaged with a few of my advisors and mentors and created a story that would help the viewer first understand what the byproduct was, follow the journey of that byproduct through our system, and eventually see how it ends up at their neighborhood grocery store. While the story was simple, it seemed promising enough to end up being what we would submit for the finals. While I would have liked more time to practice, I had only two weeks from the quarter-finals to the final pitch competition, and after ten days of rewriting and practicing, I submitted what I felt was a decent shot. On the night of the finals, we were given limited information about the setup, which was probably for the best. As I walked into the hallway that led to the green room I was given for some last-minute practice, I caught my first glimpse of the competitors in their rooms. Some seemed very relaxed and were chatting with their next-door neighbor, while a few others looked incredibly nervous, with one in particular pacing hastily back and forth in his room. Once I got to my green room, I had a few minutes to brush up on my new pitch deck before they announced that we would all need to be ready for sound check in a couple of minutes. One by one, they called us to the auditorium where we would be going on stage for the real pitch.

Walking in, I was blown away by the production effort for the evening. There were at east 20 people buzzing around, focused on who knows what. But what truly caught me off guard was the sheer size of the auditorium and how few people were in it. The organizers had booked the auditorium in the summer, assuming that Covid restrictions would have subsided by the fall. The auditorium could easily fit 750 people but was essentially empty for the evening. Additionally, due to the restrictions, all the judges were phoning in. At the end of every pitch, we couldn't see the judges; we would only hear their voices resonating into the empty auditorium. The order of the presentations was picked randomly, with Grain4Grain going in the first group of three. I already explained how fast the setup was, but actually sprinting through it all was another experience entirely. It felt like I was on stage for only 30 seconds. Once I was on stage, I had to find someone or some people to get visual feedback as I pitched because there was no audience to gauge how well my words or movement on stage were resonating. Luckily, I made eye contact with a masked audience member who I later found out, during a post-event interview, was a reporter who felt that my eye contact was entirely too much. As soon as I finished pitching, I was then left on stage to answer the questions from the judges. Unfortunately, due to the whole event being broadcasted online, there was an inevitable delay during which I would begin answering a question as the judges were impatiently asking, "Yoni, can you hear us?" This, as you can imagine, was eating away at any precious time I had left. I was able to eke out two answers before hearing "TIME" and hurried off stage so that the announcer could introduce the next contestant. With that, I was escorted to where the audience would have been seated and joined the other 20 people in the vastness of empty chairs as the next sets of contestants came and went off stage at a fairly efficient pace. What I noticed though, by the end of the last set, was that my presentation truly was something special. I never realized the power of telling stories, even after reading famed business gurus like Simon Sinek and Donald Miller. But this was the first time I realized just how potent it was. Listening to the various founders, who had amazing ideas, which in some cases, I would argue, were better than mine. When it comes to communicating those concepts, in a tight time domain, it becomes imperative that the details are left to the side, and the story of why this is important becomes the forefront.

With the last of the presenters finished, we were given a break as the online audience utilized a Facebook voting feature to nominate the first- and second-place winners, while the judges determined third through fifth. Speaking as humbly as possible, I thought we were at least a shoe-in for third place, and maybe even second. The announcer decided to name the winners from last to first. "In fifth place was" … I don't remember. The important thing was that it was not us. This meant we either didn't make the top five, which I gave a 50 per cent probability, or we were in the mix of the top four. As each place was named, I tried to act nonchalant while the other founders reacted nervously, but deep inside, I was also very nervous. The reality was that we were running out of money, and this was our chance to get some publicity and money to keep the lights on and explore the pivot I had presented on. I mentioned that the audience chose first and second place, blind to us as competitors, until the last second when the host walked on stage, marking the end of the voting session. As she pulled out the envelope to announce second place, I realized I was standing, clearly letting go of any show of confidence I had earlier. "And second place in the 2020 Tech Fuel Competition goes to…" still not Grain4Grain! I sat back in my seat, pretty distraught. I couldn't believe we didn't even place. I started texting my family and friends who voted, thank ng them and expressing some sadress that we didn't win. As I finished writing out the generic text to send to everyone, one of the producers annoyingly shook me, covered in wires and wearing a headset. I presumed he was one of the producers, and I almost angrily responded, "What are you talking about?" Before I could say anything, I heard, distantly at first, but steadily getting louder, "Grain4Grain" and the word "winner". I stopped my momentary outburst to glance at the stage, and there was the host signaling almost annoyingly for me to hurry up and get on stage. A massive check with $50,000 was written out with our "G4G" logo next to her. It finally dawned on me. We won.

I almost tripped running on stage. I shook the announcer's hand, grabbed the check, and took a few photos. All the while, I was beaming ear to ear with the disbelief that I had pulled this off. That same producer who got my attention walked on stage alongside a cameraman and conducted a brief interview with the host of the event asking questions. I wish I could remember the questions or even the contestants, but the rest of the evening was a blur. By the end of the interview, I was brought to one of the organizers of the event and was asked, "Who do we make the check out to?" Confused, I asked, "What do you mean?" They explained that because the event was delayed, the funding had already arrived, and I would receive the money that day! I told them our legal company name, signed a couple of papers, and was walking out the door with a massive check (which we still have), a trophy, and a real check for $50,000. It took me a second to compose myself, as I was alone in front of the event center in downtown San Antonio. Due to Covid, downtown felt like a ghost town. And here I was, standing with full hands walking to my car, in the emptiness of the city, realizing that what I held in my hand was a second wind to keep up the fight for accomplishing my grand vision.

2

Origin stories

Dawit and Elizabeth's escape from a communist Ethiopia— 1975 to 1982

At 12 years old, my dad, Dawit Medhin, was a young kid in war-torn Ethiopia. Generally, he would have been considered an unassuming kid: well-behaved, asked inquisitive questions, and always looking to play soccer with the neighborhood boys. Physically, nothing much has changed since then. Always the little brother in his family, he was also the shortest one in the group. But as with many kids in that era, Dawit carried a heavy heart of loss that would translate across any border as horrific. A year prior, in 1975, when he was 11 years old, the country was beginning to enter into political turmoil as the former dictator and king, Haile Selassie, was overthrown by a new political faction named the Derg. The Derg was the emerging power in a growing Marxist–Leninist era of uprisings in a variety of countries that were influenced by direct and indirect indoctrination from the Soviet Union. Similar uprisings could be witnessed all across the world, from Latin America and Southeast Asia to other countries in Africa. The people's or workers' revolutions were underway, and they were incredibly violent. This time period would add to the already astonishingly high number of people killed in the deadliest century of all time in the history of mankind. Rulers that embraced Marx and Lenin would do so with incredible cruelty, leading to the most widely recognized revolutions to this day, ranging from the ideologies of Mao and Ho Chi Minh in China and Vietnam to Castro in Cuba. In Ethiopia, a particularly gruesome individual began to emerge as the leader of the Derg party in 1974, Mengistu Mariam. His form of inciting violence in order to create the instability required to overthrow the existing monarchy was a form of political killings, torture, indiscriminate killings, and targeted propaganda.[1]

The morning that changed everything

One fateful day that year, Dawit, a friend of his, his three older sisters, and his parents were enjoying breakfast together. The prior evening, it was known that violence was beginning to spread in the city, with shooting and deathly screams being heard almost nightly. As they were eating, my dad, one of his sisters, and his mom were in a separate room when they heard a loud thud, which sounded like a door being kicked in by a boot. In almost an instinctual move, his mom moved my dad and his sister into various hiding spots in the bedroom and joined them, but at that point, the first shot had gone off. They could hear yelling and screaming in the other room and felt absolutely helpless. And as fast as it started, it ended. The soldiers could be heard yelling at each other from both the hallway and inside the room. While it was unclear what they said, they had left the home and were nowhere to be seen. His mom came out of the hiding spot first, and my dad and his sister quietly followed into the kitchen to a frightening scene. Both his father, one of his sisters, and his friend were all killed by the gunman. It was clear they needed to move quickly though, leaving the grieving for later. They did not know if this was the only time the soldiers would be coming to their home, and so within one day they moved out of their home and stayed with nearby friends who had heard about the killing. It was clear though that for my dad and his two sisters, living in that town where fighting had grown to an incredibly dangerous level, they would need to move to a different city. Within a couple weeks, my dad's mom was able to sell a large majority of their possessions and home, and used that money to help the family move to another town called Mendefera, Eritrea, where they would stay for a month.

Now, my dad's story, and in many ways my own too, is evidence of both the power of faith and the power of community. To many, faith is an abstract concept associated with belief in some sort of deity or deities. Faith, in the presence of great trauma and hopelessness, is the fuel for perseverance. It helps people make it through incredibly dark times and the worst of situations. Community, when expressed appropriately, is the sharing of burdens and victories with each other. It's the authentic connection that helps one maintain faith to continue persevering in life. When one member of the community reaches the mountaintop, they all experience the victory. And when one is in the depth of despair, the community helps carry a portion of the burden to lift them up.

My dad is great in many ways, but he will be the first to tell you that he is a product of his community. He was the product of many people throughout his life who contributed to his eventual success many decades later. From people praying for him, to people giving him and his family shelter as they continued to escape the ensuing war, to people advising him to make it out West where democracy and opportunity lie. As my dad and his remaining family were making it through the first year after the killings, the fighting began expanding into neighboring cities, including the secluded towns where they were staying. Once again, for the safety of the children, my grandma was searching for a way out. A distant cousin of my dad, who would later also settle in the United States, had heard about the killings from others a few weeks after the incident. He quickly began following their footsteps from town to town via word of mouth for a few weeks. Communications were sparse at the time, with no cellphones or emails to reach them. From his point of view, which was informed by news stations like the BBC and other programs that were tracking the now escalating uprisings in the region, the family needed to relocate to a new city. There, they would find some more stability to begin rebuilding some semblance of a life. My dad's cousin knew that it would be extremely difficult to travel by car to their destination, as all the major roadways had blockades where people were being routinely killed or hauled off into prisons. So they decided to travel by foot for several days to bypass the major blockades and make it into the main city centers. After mulling over the risks, which ranged from being caught by a patrol unit to dying from the elements like the heat or wild animals, they decided that if they were to stay where they were, the fighting could escalate and trap them. So my grandma rounded up her three remaining children, strapped the money they had left to her undergarments and her body in case they were stopped, and with the little belongings they had, they were led by my dad's cousin across the wilderness for three days.

During the journey, their biggest worry became a reality: patrollers were able to find them. But in the wisdom of my grandma, she had taped the money to her body, preventing them from finding anything within their belongings. They were allowed to pass to the next town unharmed. While this stark example may have been good fortune, to my family and me, this is just a small glimpse of the providence and protection that would be a theme in my family's story for the next several decades. The town they settled in, in the Tigray region of Ethiopia, was called Adi Tigrat.

Once there, they settled into a new home with the money saved up and began rebuilding their life, one day at a time. My dad was able to attend a Catholic boarding school which, after they heard about his ordeal the last couple of months, was free for him to attend. Keep in mind, he had not been attending school for the last two to three months and, worried he would fall behind, his cousin was urging that he go back to school in whatever way he could. My dad's sister was still in shock, but she was able to return to some semblance of a life and worked a bit here and there. And this was their life for a few years—they had some momentary peace and time to grieve. My dad was able to have some stability, which allowed him to begin excelling in school. My grandma had to assume the role of both parents, which is obviously hard in any context, but being widowed and losing children makes it an especially jarring reality. However, and as is still the case today, she was sharp and very wise. She made sure her remaining kids were taken care of and was prepared to make any necessary sacrifices.

My father's escape out of the country through education

As the fighting escalated, it became apparent that their town may succumb to the war next. Things began to slowly shift in areas where the war grew. For those aware of how towns changed during World War II and the Nazi expansion, towns would first start to lose people going out to fight the war. Then certain high-profile or powerful people would begin to turn in favor of the opposition or leave the city. From there, with resources and people slowly depleting, a town was ripe for takeover.

This was being experienced within Adi Tigrat as the fighting started to escalate in the outer regions of the city. More and more of the city's protective service members were being sent to fight, leaving the town defenseless. It became so bad that, at one point, they handed my dad a rifle and made him patrol the school at night, forcing him to walk around the perimeter until sunrise. However, as the fighting grew worse, it was the Ethiopian communists that were gathering young boys to shoot. My dad would recall a battle against the Liberation Front, where they trained him and his friend for three weeks on basic combat, and then trucked them out to battle. My dad was incredibly distraught by this and immediately began searching for a way out of the city before he would be sent out to fight again. His older sister worked for the Ministry of Agriculture and, in secret, helped my dad get processed for a school transfer to Addis Ababa. The timing was unbelievable. Once my dad's transfer was complete, he received word within a couple weeks that his friend was killed in a battle, along with many other young boys. While the city of Addis Ababa had undergone a communist uprising, it was still relatively safe compared to other cities in Ethiopia and Eritrea. The family had a distant relative in Addis Ababa, Ethiopia, who would also immigrate to the United States. They agreed to take my dad in until he finished his last two years of high school at the age of 18. So, at the age of 16, my dad would be separated from his family and would not resume any extended period of time with them for the rest of his life.

Addis Ababa at the time was more stable compared to other cities undergoing conflict, but it was far from an easy life. An example of just how difficult the environment was to learn in is that, due to limited resources and availability of material (e.g., textbooks), limits were imposed for accessing the library materials. For example, say you were preparing for a chemistry exam. Unless you were wealthy and had the disposable income to buy a copy of the book, you were forced to wait for the next available one at the library. Usually there would be a long line at the library to check out the book, and there was a time limit for using the book. Additionally, because of the scarcity of material, they would not allow you to leave the library with the book. So here's my dad and several other students, preparing for an exam and only being allowed to check out a book for a couple of hours. While this situation would be untenable in the United States, the reality forced the students to savor their study time and maximize any time they had. There are many examples of the scarcity my family and so many others in that time period experienced. My dad had excelled time and time again, and when it was time for the university entrance exams, he would perform well in those too. For many, the exams were simply a way to continue schooling within Ethiopia, and more commonly, one of the universities in

Addis Ababa. My dad, and several others, looked to the exams as a way out. The mechanics of trying to get out were tricky and very risky. Once you took the test, you were allowed to do one of two things—either use the score and submit it to a university within the country or take the chance to forgo that and see if a university in a different country would take you in. Here is where it became risky: you couldn't change your mind if you didn't get accepted abroad and try to resubmit your scores to an Ethiopian university.

This was a mutually exclusive decision.

At the time, the Soviet Union, while showing signs of disruption and instability internally, was still far and away the other superpower of the world. And, most impressively, their universities had surpassed the United States in several categories within STEM fields. The USSR at the time had signed numerous agreements since the end of World War II with various countries in the Horn of Africa. The agreements resulted in hundreds of millions of dollars (adjusted for inflation today) helping with a variety of categories, including agriculture, military training and bolstering, infrastructure, and education. As part of these agreements, the USSR agreed to train several hundred thousand people in Africa and also agreed to train and educate Africans within their own universities. Most of these students would study in STEM fields for five years, receive a master's degree, and return to their countries. The program, in the Soviets' eyes, served multiple purposes. One, the United States had already begun conducting operations in Africa and other regions that began to be heavily influenced by the Soviets after World War II. This was a way to not only fight the United States in the form of a proxy but also to win the hearts of the countries they were in. This did not always work out—think Afghanistan and other countries in that region where the instability of the two world powers' interference still continues to bring echoes of the past turmoil today. But in many cases, the programs worked to help build the USSR's international influence and turn the tide in many cases in their favor. Cuba, Vietnam, Ethiopia, etc. are all examples of this being done remarkably well.[2]

For students like my dad, there were limited spots to get into one of these programs. So, my dad put his name into the ring and opted to go to the USSR if his test scores were selected. Every year, they would only select a few hundred students out of the thousands that took the university entrance exams. To reiterate, if you were not selected, you would be unable to continue on to university for a whole year. While the risk was there, my dad was confident he would be selected—and selected he was! I can only imagine the feeling after all the years since his dad died and coming to this moment where he would finally have an opportunity to do something meaningful with his life. There were other motivations for going to Moscow as well. He had become a Christian a couple years back and knew that communism was highly hostile to his newfound faith. He also had aspirations of succeeding in business or some form of owning property, and that too was treated hostilely under communism. At least in Russia there would be a chance to escape to Europe because it was close by; whereas, in Ethiopia, the chance of getting out without any support was near impossible. A few years later, one of my dad's sisters attempted to cross into Sudan in order to escape the violence, and would sadly end up dying because of hunger and exposure to the harsh desert environment. So, with no other choices for a better life present, he moved to Moscow for the start of his education in the USSR.

My mother's escape from the country to the West

Now, my mom's story is thankfully less traumatic than my dad's but is also fraught with grief. As a young teenager growing up in Addis Ababa, there were not many options for future growth and potential as a woman. While women were able to grow in professional careers, it was very rare, even after the communist regime took over. During that time in the city, as earlier described, various officers and party enforcers would shut down businesses and other private entities as they would either become controlled by the central party or be removed altogether. There was also the beginning of a war against the region up north, which would soon become Eritrea. The communist party began killing and imprisoning people that were Eritrean as a way to protect their power. My mom was one of six kids in her family, and her dad worked as a truck driver in the city. Her family was Eritrean and had moved to Addis prior to when she was born. When the communist regime began its crackdown, they found out my grandfather was placed in prison for three years as a form of intimidation. At the time, there were no official ways of leaving the country, meaning going through a designated port where you are checked prior to leaving (e.g., airport, port of entry for a car or ship, or train station). Most people would escape in caravans that were usually on foot or through smuggling routes. Others would lie upon leaving certain ports and would not return to their country, claiming asylum or some sort of refugee status when arriving in another country. When my grandfather was placed in prison, my mom's older siblings scattered across various neighboring countries as they found their way west. Her eldest brother, who currently resides in Virginia, was able to escape to Italy. Two of her sisters were able to escape through Nairobi, Kenya, and eventually made their way to the United States, where one resides in North Carolina and the other in Texas; and one brother eventually settled in Toronto, Canada Before my mom graduated from high school, her grandfather was released from prison, and after some time with him and the remaining family in Addis, she would end up leaving for Italy in order to join her older brother as she would look to find her way westward toward North America. Once in Italy, my mom began working as a nanny and lived at a monastery for a year before being able to receive asylum in Ottawa, Canada.

3
The problem

A unique attempt at solving the problem of food waste in the US—2016 to 2017

As a college student, I was not particularly known as a hard worker. I was lucky that the last half of my undergrad experience was relatively easy, allowing me to get a 4.0 most semesters, which balanced out my poor performances in my earlier years. However, during my internships, I realized that school was merely a check in the box, and the real world was incredibly different. Once I got a taste of how things really operated, I wanted to get out of school fast. So, I worked with my advisors to come up with a course layout that would allow me to graduate in three years. But, as fate would have it, the rules of the game changed at the last minute. I would have to take a course during a fourth year because it was no longer offered in both semesters, leaving me with a very barren schedule. Despite this, I had already secured a high-paying job for when I graduated with the company I had interned for, so I took the time to enjoy doing the things I wanted to do. I skied, camped, trail ran, traveled, and took electives that interested me, one of which was a business course called Entrepreneurship. Entrepreneurship was the type of class you take when you are trying to coast through your last semester in college, and I was guilty as charged. When we began the class, we were tasked by the professors to come up with an idea that we would take to the MVP (Minimum Viable Product) stage by the end of the semester. We would organize a founding team, conduct market research, develop a prototype, and present it to a group of actual angel investors from a local network. This course was not very prescriptive as they were attempting to really get the students to think creatively from ground zero, but they would provide a series of literature and lectures at the various stages of development to help contextualize the project to a potential real-world application.

I had a few friends from a campus Bible study and some buddies I skied with in the class, so naturally we formed a team. Everyone on the team had jobs already lined up, so it made the class very difficult at first to take seriously—especially when most of the grade was attendance and the final project. As we started the first few weeks, we listened and read some standard materials ranging from Steve Jobs' origins to learning the Why from Simon Sinek. What actually began to pique my interest was some of the auxiliary material we were given to help understand a startup business model. As I learned what a startup is, I began to put that into the context of my family, some folks I looked up to that had graduated from Mines in years past, and even the corporations my classmates were vying to get offers from. I started to see and understand a key point: entrepreneurship was the backbone of industry. And, even more intriguing to me, was that it is incredibly hard, and risky, but on the off chance it works out (depending on the definition of success, which we will get back to), remarkably rewarding.

As a Christian who genuinely seeks to improve people's lives instead of pursuing wealth, I believed that any project we worked on would need to serve a tangible need and have a real, measurable impact on people's lives. These guidelines were the approach I took within the group as we searched for ideas. One evening, a group member was brewing beer and recommended that I try it out. The following weekend, I went with a girl I had dated in college to a local brewery that offered patrons the opportunity to brew their own beer recipe with the guidance of one of the owners. For my birthday, I brewed a very hazy IPA for my rugby team. During the brewing process, we were able to select the malts, hops, and even the level of alcohol range depending on the available yeasts.

Stumbling into upcycling

In the first few weeks of my entrepreneurship class, I spent a weekend learning about spent grain after my little brewing project. While in class the following week, one of our teammates, who was a real amateur brewer with a full home kit, mentioned that he would normally utilize the grain at home when making bread or pizza. I asked him what he normally did with the grains, and he said he would throw them out or leave them out for people to take for animal feed. To my amazement, he had just frozen some grain in small batches, and offered to give me some. I headed home from campus with about five pounds of frozen spent grain, googling on my phone the best methods to dry spent grain at home. The easiest option I found was to dry the grain utilizing an oven that had a convection fan, leaving it open a crack to allow the grain to air out and not build up humidity in the oven. These tips helped guide my research in later years on drying efficiency and led to our current iteration of drying food byproducts.

With an oven pan handy, I spread the grain out in a thin layer, turned the oven on at the lowest temperature setting with a six-hour timer, and allowed the grain to fully dry without compromising the flavor from burning. Once dried, the grain resembled a very dry granola base at first glance and had a decent taste, almost like a rustic oat flavor. I spent the weekend searching for some of the easiest home recipes that would help accentuate the flavors and give the product some life. Landing on a fruity granola cereal mix, I began to tinker with the grain. After a few iterations over the weekend, I landed on a pretty tasty cereal that would act as our first product iteration to present in our entrepreneurship class.

To my surprise, my roommates really enjoyed the beer granola mix, so I packaged a few samples to see if people would be willing to purchase it. People were happy to buy it for a few dollars, and some of the ingredients included blueberries, coconuts, a variety of nuts, and honey to bind it all together. After a few sales, our team iterated another product, a peanut butter granola bar, and with the two products in tow, we were off to the races in creating some business models around them. The class was set up so that, on a bi-weekly basis, we would get up in front of everyone and share our progress as it corresponded with the different themes of developing a business from the ground up. In this particular presentation, our team began to describe the process of developing the grain and flour to make our food products (granola and energy bars), and another student wisely asked why we didn't just act as an ingredient supplier and then offload the hard work of making a brand and associated products.

This insight was key to helping us realize a few specific problems in the space of "upcycling" byproducts from food manufacturers. The first insight was the production challenge of creating ingredients from these byproducts. If you've ever brewed beer or made any beverage that requires extraction (e.g., juicing, nut milk, etc.), there are several waste streams. One of these is the pulp or mash that originates from the wort, which is a concentrated sugar water or concentrate. Additionally, waste streams may include steam if there is a boiling step in the process and any flavorings along the way. Waste streams for beer production are largely concentrated within one stream: the grain output, commonly known as "spent grain". "Spent" refers to the grain after it has been expended of its carbohydrate-rich starches, which would later be consumed by yeast for the production of alcohol and some carbon dioxide. This process in brewing is known as "mashing"—where the grain is boiled to extract the water-soluble starches.

The basics of upcycling

The process leaves behind a moisture-bound grain that mostly consists of fiber and protein, depending on how efficient the extraction process is. Here's a sample equation to help describe what's happening in order to produce this waste stream:

1. Barley grain goes into boiling water.

    a. Barley is made up of 70 per cent carbohydrates, 20 per cent fiber, and 10 per cent protein (just an example).

    b.   Let's say you have 1 g of barley going into hot water, and that 1 g is broken up into the percentages from above. It would look like this:

        i.   0.7 g of carbs + 0.2 g of fiber + 0.1 g of protein + 1 g of water (equal parts water for the example).

2.   Once the grain is done mashing and nearly all the carbohydrates have been extracted, you're left with the following in the waste stream:

    a.   0.7 g of water + 0.2 g of fiber + 0.1 g of protein (again, very rough math).

If you noticed, the water is replacing the carbohydrate by weight. This is because barley is an incredibly fibrous grain that allows it to hold on to water. As the carbohydrates dissolve in the water, they get replaced by the water. This is a huge challenge for large corporations when attempting to commercialize spent grain in production. The grain is not only coming out of the process extremely wet (greater than 70 per cent moisture content) but it is also very volatile due to the heavy organics and bioactivity in the process. Concerns about rapid spoilage and health risks have always presented a hurdle when looking to create some sort of food product with spent grain and byproducts as a whole category. When you have a product that is additionally coming out of a process that is hot (present in most beverage manufacturing), the spoilage is kicked up rapidly.

There are only two options to pause or stop spoilage in the byproduct stream. Option 1 is to freeze the grain. Unfortunately, the level of energy required to freeze something so dense and warm is very inefficient relative to what you would be getting. Additionally, the grain would still need to be turned into something shelf-stable. This leads us to option 2, which is shelf-stabilizing the grain. This can be done by one of two ways (generally). The first is to stop the growth of microorganisms through a process that sterilizes the grain so that it can remain wet but not be nearly as bioactive. The second option is to dry the grain. By drying it to a moisture level under 10 per cent, the grain will be able to reach shelf stability, like the bag of rice or oats in your pantry. Remember, we started at 70 per cent moisture. The challenge with drying is twofold. One, there are many options for drying something, and two, not all those options are very energy or cost-efficient. It's challenging to find something that is both energy and cost-efficient from the variety of options out there.

Another insight we gathered after our classmate brought up the idea of converting to just an ingredient supplier was the use cases for the ingredient itself. It was clear that the whole grain had some easy applications for our snacks and breakfast products, but as a flour, there were vastly more product inclusion opportunities. While this was past our product development phase for the class, we utilized that concept for the pitch at the end of the class to the board of investors from whom our final grade would be provided. It was clear during the pitch that the concept of utilizing the unique technology to make a product with a wide range of applicability resonated the most.

After the pitches, we received our final grade the week of graduation. With an A in hand, I walked across the aisle, grabbed my diploma, and was off to go on a month-long backpacking trip before being consigned to my first engineering job in North Dakota.

Working my first "big boy" job

The company I was employed at, Hess Corporation, had a unique program where they would routinely move us around the various business units to get a broad view of how the company operated in the United States. My rotations were only centered around United States business assets, which were primarily officed out of North Dakota and Houston. Around month four, I was given an assignment in Houston.

When you get your first "real job" after college, you realize a few key things. First, almost everything you learned in school is not applicable. Some of the first projects I was assigned during my training rotational program were all things you just have to learn while on the job. Most of the systems, methodologies, and metrics that were used to evaluate projects had no relationship to what I was learning in college. Second, office politics really matter, especially at larger firms. While being a solid engineer mattered, the corporate world was less of a meritocracy and more of a popularity contest. Being good enough at the work and being well-liked were the most important combo for succeeding. Lastly, only a few people are having their time 100 per cent utilized. In an eight- to nine-hour workday, most people are only working 60 to 70 per cent of the time. High achievers would be looking throughout their day to pick up more projects, while most others are cruising through the workweek. These are all generalizations, of course, but they were the reality I experienced as I began working in the corporate world.

In Houston, at the company headquarters, I was given a rotation within the business unit as an economist. The role would essentially be an analyst-type role where I would utilize my engineering skill set to help provide leadership with a better understanding of the impacts of various decisions. Some examples would be M&A deals, where I would provide constraint analysis and basic economic evaluation as we looked to purchase pipelines around the country. Some would be large-scale, $1 billion projects that I would help provide analysis for, using some programming I was beginning to learn on the job.

As projects would come and go, I began to realize a fact that was true almost ubiquitously across most companies and industries: business and the business leaders of a corporation are actually the real decision-makers. It may seem overly obvious to most, but when you are an engineer, you are usually siloed and constrained to defined projects and objectives that oddly mimic boundaries in many ways. These boundaries restrict an engineer from being exposed to and actually seeing the big picture. To most, no one really cares, as engineers are usually compensated well relative to the rest of the company for their skill set and line of work. For some, including me, once exposed to the big picture, or at least a portion of it, and a realization of how decisions are trickled down to what would become projects for, say, a new engineer out of college, ambition kicks in to be that decision-maker. It was for the first time, almost as a revelation, that I saw how business was really the engine for how things work within the economy.

For so long, I was told that engineers were "smarter than business people" and that our work "mattered more" because we were working on tangible things that shaped the world. In my naivety, I took them at their word. Business was something that I had neglected but was quickly getting a crash course on in Houston. I was beginning to see that, while engineers are vital in building and maintaining infrastructure, it is ultimately the business leaders who decide what gets built in the first place. They assess market forces, societal needs, available technology, cost constraints, and a myriad of other factors to determine where capital should be allocated. Though I had scoffed at "silly" business courses during college, I now saw them as the key to understanding value creation and how the world operates. My engineering skills would be rendered useless without the business acumen to apply them effectively. This realization instilled in me a newfound respect for the business side and a hunger to bridge the gap between the technical and the strategic. I hoped one day to bring an engineer's analytical abilities to evaluating opportunities and managing operations.

4

Coming to (North) America

How our family made it to the West looking to start a new journey—1982 to 1991

In Moscow, my dad had spent almost six months there going through an indoctrination, language program, and a prerequisite program prior to starting his undergraduate and master's degrees. When placing students around the country, the USSR had specific regions for specific types of education. Engineers, doctors, scientists, and liberal arts students all studied in separate universities around the entire country. The USSR had selected my dad to study agricultural engineering, which most closely translates to civil engineering with a small mix of mechanical engineering. The region my dad was sent to was Tashkent, Uzbekistan. There he would be required to spend the next five to six years studying under the communist regime various communist philosophies alongside his engineering degree. When reading through various history books you will find that the USSR, while lacking in many things relative to the other superpower at the time, the United States, did not lack in education specifically within STEM fields. Regardless of having that knowledge, my dad had already set his sights on finding his way to America. He knew he did not want to stay in Europe largely because the economy in the United States, he knew, would provide vastly more opportunities for having some semblance of a financially stable life than in the USSR or Ethiopia, where he was expected to be sent back to upon completing his education in the USSR.

My dad began to search for opportunities to defect from the country. He knew of several people who had been able to do it in the past just through stories and word of mouth. However, while the stories were there and examples of people successfully escaping were known, the opportunities were incredibly slim. He knew that the only way to be able to escape would have to be during a vacation. During the time when the USSR was bringing foreign students into the country for education, all the while the nation was being ravaged by various famines and other economically distressing events, the foreigners were given vastly more privileges and resources than those around them. Already with a disdain for communism after seeing what happened in Ethiopia, my dad was well aware that the image presented to him along with all the other foreign students was a facade. For example, while the students were in school they would get access to various types of technologies, which at the time were considered extravagant. These included access to radios, some TVs, and even different types of clothing including jeans and nice shirts. More importantly, they never had to worry about food, room, or board. All of that was provided to the students in order to continue preserting this utopic image of communism from the main driving ergine in the world.

As a part of these favors and handouts to the foreign students, vacations were offered after a couple years into their university studies. Many students would usually just venture back to Moscow, which was very beautiful as it was the pinnacle city within the USSR. Others would explore various areas within Eastern Europe, including Prague, Czechoslovakia, Warsaw, Crimea, Kiev, and East Berlin. Additionally, the USSR would also allow the students to cross the Berlin Wall into West Germany, only during their vacation period, so that they could go and spend some of their money acquiring some of the things in West Berlin. To this day I can only really pinpoint the reason why they would even allow such a policy, their willingness to let students go into what in all sense of the words would be enemy territory, as probably some misguided pride in their own facade, believing no one would ever actually want to leave the country and defect—especially the foreign students, who were leaving incredibly dire circumstances back home and were given so much favor within the USSR.

Escaping the Soviet Union

My dad knew that the opportunities for vacations were so rare, that he was determined to leave on the first chance he got. So when his time was up at his university in Uzbekistan, he received a permit allowing him to travel within the country back to Moscow. Leaving all his possessions behind except for two bags and his winter hat, and only a couple weeks of time, he decided to make his way to Prague in order to see if there were some avenues to make it toward East Berlin, where he believed he would be able to find help after crossing the Berlin Wall. To his incredible fortune, he met an Eritrean man in the town of Old Prague after spending just less than one day there. This man was actually someone wanted by the Ethiopian communist army, as he was part of the Liberation Front primarily made up of Eritreans, who would later achieve their independence when Eritrea became a sovereign nation in the 1990s. He was considered a war criminal and my dad would recount stories of attempted kidnappings by the Ethiopian Communist Party in order to bring him to the country for trial and likely his execution.

So when my dad met this man, he was still basically in hiding, minimizing contact with other Eritreans within the USSR, and other areas in Europe, and back home. However, he had already assisted people in crossing the Berlin Wall, and knew of another Eritrean man who had established a home and a medical practice in West Berlin, and recommended that my dad find this man as soon as he could make it to West Berlin in order to assist in his defection and processing to make it to a Western country. So my dad spent the next two to three days traveling by night, in order to avoid suspicion and questioning from the army and other officers of the USSR, made his way to East Berlin, and walked across toward West Berlin. I already mentioned that they had already established a program for these foreign students to be able to go relatively freely. So when my dad arrived, they did not check his permit, which only showed that he was supposed to be in Moscow or Prague, let him walk across, and my dad never returned again.

Keep in mind he is only 20 at this point. I have to ask, what were you doing at the age of 20? I can tell you I was not escaping a communist country, looking for economic opportunities in the West. I was likely eating pizza with friends after a day of skiing. When my dad arrived in West Berlin, he found some local Eritreans nearby, and met with this doctor, who was overjoyed at the news that my dad had been able to meet with his former contact in Old Prague. They immediately began work on his defection, working closely with the German government established at the time to help him process his asylum within West Berlin, and to also begin the process of seeking asylum in the United States.

With the help of Caritas, a Catholic non-profit serving refugees across the world. he was able to apply for and receive permanent resident status within the United States, under a green card. The whole immigration process took six months, and so during that time my dad played for a semi-pro soccer team, as he was still in relatively good shape at the time, learned more language, primarily German, and expanded his knowledge of his still relatively new faith. Caritas had a fund available for people looking to make it to the United States by plane, and ended up purchasing my dad's ticket to Denver via TWA. In Denver, my dad's cousin, who had originally allowed him to stay with them in Addis Ababa, had already settled in Denver, and helped my dad by hosting his visa.

My father's arrival in the United States of America

As a freshly minted 21-year-old, on the evening of September 28, 1984, my dad first stepped foot in Denver International Airport, finally in the United States. When interviewing him for this story, he told me the first thought that came to his mind was that it felt like home as soon as he got here. My dad was hungry to get started working, and wanted to begin building his life here.

His cousin had three kids and a small house, but they still were able to get my dad a room. And within a few weeks my dad began supporting himself, working as a pharmaceutical technician making $3.20 per hour. Once he was able to start working he wanted to get out of his cousin's hair as he was also plenty busy with raising his family. My dad had another cousin who was coming from Sudan after escaping the country and immigrating to the United States as a refugee after finding that my dad and his cousin were here as well. So once his cousin arrived and began work, they decided to move into a small apartment, where my dad still recalls the rent: $320 per month. I'd love to expand on all the stories, and if you ever get the opportunity to meet my dad, please ask him about this time when he first made it to the United States, experiencing so many adventures trying to learn about this country, learning the language, and establishing a community he is still deeply committed to.

In 1984, my mom was in Italy, living at a monastery, as they were housing her for free at the time, and working as a nanny in order to make ends meet. During that year my mom was also looking to make it to North America. Still young, but ambitious, she knew that making it to the West would also provide her more opportunities than in Europe. So she applied for asylum to the first country that would grant it, which ended up being Canada. She knew that there were Ethiopians in Ottawa, so she chose Ottawa as her place to immigrate to. By 1985 she was granted asylum, was given a plane ticket, and flew to Canada. When she arrived she began work as a security guard, in order to make ends meet. While she did not expand on this, my assumption is that there were other Ethiopians working as security guards, and that the Ethiopian community is very communal in ways that expand to style of work and professions, where people end up living, and the other places they congregate and gather. My mom has a knack for detail and hard work, so she got admission to Ottawa College and began studying accounting. Her goal was to graduate in four or five years, get a job, and begin building a life in Canada. At the time she too was very focused on her community and faith, something my dad and mom have in common. So she began a small fellowship with other Ethiopian friends in the hope of starting a church. During this time, she would have to wait until 1991 for her citizenship to be granted in Canada.

5
The solution

Using first principles to create our invention and the foundation for our business— 2017 to spring 2018

While in Houston, the economics desk went through regular fluctuations in workload. These periods of heightened productivity typically lasted three to five weeks, depending on the project, followed by a temporary lull of about two to three weeks until the next deal or major assignment was assigned to the team for analysis. The work was genuinely captivating, and truth be told, had I been given the opportunity to continue with the group, I might not have embarked on the Grain4Grain venture; or, at the very least, I would have delayed its initiation. Projects ranged from intricate optimization challenges involving multiple variables, where I developed production schedules for significant assets based on predicted capacities, to refining and selling the resulting products. At times, I assumed the role of a statistician, running sensitivity analyses on potential projects and asset mergers and acquisitions. One particular project involved examining sales prices of large assets and employing various methods to determine an expected value that helped assess whether the asking or selling price was adequate or disadvantageous. In rare cases, we uncovered instances of overpayment, in which my group would provide reasoning as to why a deal should be pursued or not. One of the additional perks of the job was its cross-functional nature, allowing me to interact with individuals from various departments within the oil and gas industry. I began to appreciate the significance of other functions within this world, such as the land department, which acted as our business development team, primary negotiators, and initial investment managers; the data analytics team, which offered valuable tools for decision-making across multiple functions; the engineers, who drove development and design; and the geologists, who were responsible for exploration and identifying new assets. The intricate complexity of having all these groups collaborate within the organization fascinated me. Together, we fulfilled the role of internal economic consultants. The organization had several other groups at a central level that provided consultancy services for different initiatives. Examples of such groups included marketing (mainly commodity sales) and technical teams, which were often focused on major engineering projects.

During the initial cycles of productivity and downtime in our group, I utilized the downtime to explore the organization and gain a deeper understanding of its various components. On occasion, I was fortunate enough to contribute in various capacities as time allowed. While this occupied most of my week, my weekends were primarily spent ruminating over the idea of entrepreneurship and, more importantly, addressing the challenge of upcycling spent grain. I started taking extended lunch breaks to engage in conversations with different breweries in Houston's city center, aiming to gain a comprehensive understanding of how each brewery managed its byproduct waste and disposal practices. After a couple of weeks of using my lunch breaks to visit breweries, I decided to pick up where I had left off with the idea back in college. The first step was to acquire some spent grain. I needed a dried product at hand, preferably in flour form, to proceed further. As you may recall, the available method for drying spent grain involved using a kitchen oven as a makeshift dehydrator. To effectively test various milling solutions and later explore potential applications, I needed a few pounds of dried spent grain. Given my limited time and initial scope, I postponed the search for a drying solution and focused on obtaining the initial product to experiment with. Thus began a month-long project of using my weekday lunches to bring Tupperware to work, going on extended breaks to arrange for a small pick-up of spent grain from local breweries, rushing home to begin dehydrating the spent grain in the oven, and then returning to work while the grain dried in the oven at home. By the end of the first day, my apartment mate complained about the combined aroma of a bakery and brewery lingering in our living space. By the fourth day of the home dehydration project, I overheard someone in the lobby lamenting that their penthouse suite smelled like a brewery. While unintended, I couldn't help but find it amusing. Throughout the month, I also embarked on the task of experimenting with milling brewers' spent grain. There are a few notable characteristics of this ingredient compared to more conventional grains. One key distinction is its significantly higher fiber content, as discussed in Chapter 3, which can be attributed to the mashing process and the subsequent removal of carbohydrates.

My exploration of entrepreneurship

There are numerous essential qualities that define an entrepreneur. Beyond the necessary dose of naivety and risk tolerance, we encounter common characteristics such as resourcefulness, frugality, vision, drive, and so forth—the list is extensive. However, it is rare for entrepreneurs to possess all the necessary traits and strengths to be entirely self-reliant; they often require a team. Yet finding like-minded individuals can be a challenging task. Team-building can be pursued through various methods, but two main approaches come to mind—ones that I contemplated during the early stages while still tinkering with the solution to the problem of food waste at Hess.

The first approach revolves around the idea or problem itself, with efforts focused on solving problems by seeking individuals who can effectively address those needs. Here is a basic framework, along with an example: let's consider Company ABC, which has noticed a decline in sales within a particular sector. Recognizing that a combination of renewed marketing efforts and fresh designs could fuel the desired growth, Company ABC logically embarks on a quest to either find suitable individuals within the organization or hire external talents to tackle the task at hand. Allow me to provide a few examples and references to illustrate this approach.

Say that Apple wants to launch a new "iCar", and they decide the best way to approach this is by hiring the best and brightest car designers, engineers, and marketers for this new product. By doing this, the in effect outsource the expertise externally in order to bridge the business need they have determined. The problem comes first, the people are brought in second.

Now back to our former example of Apple, the way a people-centric approach would play out could look something like this. Apple looks for the most talented people from various sectors and disciplines. Out of their creativity, and through proper motivation and incentives, they look to develop a new product to meet a current, or not-yet-realized, need. They decide to create an "iCar", seeing that the market would benefit, and so would Apple, from creating a new market for 'smart cars", or something like that.

On the other hand, people-centric methods take a vastly different approach. In this scenario, the central ideator, be it a corporation or the entrepreneur themselves, seeks out exceptionally intelligent individuals and relies on their expertise to find the best solutions to problems. At this point, the entrepreneur or business leader's role shifts to maintaining guardrails, providing clear definitions of success, and fostering thoughtful communication. Once these fundamentals are in place, the next, and perhaps most critical, step is for the entrepreneur to take a back seat and let these brilliant individuals unleash their potential.

A great and not so well known business decision-making process, similar to the approach of "people centric" problem solving and decision making, is "effectuation". Effectuation is a decision-making framework that is often used in entrepreneurship and business contexts. It was introduced by Saras Sarasvathy, a professor at the University of Virginia's Darden School of Business. The concept of effectuation contrasts with traditional approaches to decision-making that rely on predicting and analyzing future outcomes (Sarasvathy, 2001).

In effectuation, entrepreneurs start with their available means (resources, skills, and networks) and focus on what they can control in the present moment. They take action, experiment, and adapt based on feedback and opportunities that arise. Rather than attempting to predict the future or analyze market trends, effectuation emphasizes leveraging existing resources to create new possibilities and shape the future through a process of "making it up as you go".

Effectuation principles include:

- Bird-in-Hand Principle: Start with what you have. Entrepreneurs leverage their existing resources, skills, and networks to create opportunities.
- Affordable Loss Principle: Take calculated risks. Instead of solely focusing on potential rewards, entrepreneurs consider what they can afford to lose and make decisions accordingly.
- Crazy Quilt Principle: Form partnerships. Entrepreneurs collaborate with others, building mutually beneficial relationships and assembling a network of supporters.
- Lemonade Principle: Embrace surprises. Entrepreneurs remain open to unexpected outcomes and view them as potential sources of opportunity.
- Pilot-in-the-Plane Principle: Maintain control. Entrepreneurs believe in their ability to shape the future through their actions and decisions.

- Effectuation is particularly relevant in uncertain and dynamic environments, where traditional forecasting and planning may be less effective. It provides a flexible and adaptive approach to entrepreneurship and innovation[3] (Sarasvathy, 2001).

All of the above is easier said than done. While these ideas had been formulating in my mind as a young and budding entrepreneur, it takes more discipline than I had initially developed to fully benefit from these fundamental concepts in the early days of my first venture. As the concept of upcycling began to take hold, a significant issue emerged—a marketplace for this product, when most "upcycled" products had yet to materialize. In 2018, only a small handful of businesses had even sold products utilizing upcycled ingredients. In the process of effectuation and attempting to solve a smaller problem first, it became evident that the marketplace was too important to ignore.

Finding a co-founder and defining what our business would be

Enter my first co-founder, Matt. Now, Matt is an extraordinary individual. He possesses a brilliant analytical mind when it comes to gathering data and, more importantly, identifying themes and utilizing them to construct simple and coherent lines of thought. Moreover, he happened to be my first friend in college. I vividly remember the nervousness I felt as I walked through the halls of Mines on my first day. There was an event hosted where all the clubs and organizations showcased their activities on campus. And there was Matt, hosting a booth for a Bible study group, which I later joined. Coincidentally, he was wearing a rugby t-shirt that

I owned (it was almost like a friendship written in the stars). We became friends through shared majors, playing rugby together for a few years, and attending numerous events side by side.

Five years later, Matt, who had been working in Houston in a similar analytics role for a different company, reached out to me, and we reconnected. Interestingly, on one of the very first nights we hung out, I was drying grain in my apartment kitchen oven. I showed Matt the concept and the various iterations I had gone through in both drying the grain and attempting to mill it into usable flour. That night, before his arrival, I had breaded tilapia using the initial version of the flour. Matt was astounded and uttered an iconic line, "Do you realize what you've done?" It's worth noting that Matt, an amateur nutrition scientist and bodybuilder, had delved into understanding the effects of macronutrients on the body, its composition, and performance. He had spent considerable time documenting his diet and observing his physique change in response to specific dietary modifications. If you recall, brewers' spent grain is primarily carbohydrate-depleted due to the mashing process during brewing. Matt immediately recognized a market opportunity for the flour within the bodybuilding community (or anyone seeking to minimize carb intake).

Initially, I had viewed this ingredient from a more altruistic standpoint—a solution to address sustainability concerns within the food ecosystem. However, Matt brought up a valid point by referring to Maslow's hierarchy of needs. This hierarchy ranks needs from direct survival essentials (such as food, water, and shelter) to less immediate priorities like caring for others or the environment. Effective consumer marketing must tap into multiple layers of needs. A notable example of this implementation is Simon Sinek's "Golden Circle". The Golden Circle consists of three concentric circles (see Figure 1), with the most crucial part being the center, labeled as "why", and expanding outward to the less significant components of "how" and "what". When focusing on the "why" aspect, Simon often mentions Apple and their range of consumer hardware products. He explains that Apple successfully taps into a deep-seated need for individuals to feel both unique and connected. Apple products transcend being mere handheld devices or laptops; they provide a premium experience of belonging and "coolness". This aspect addresses a fundamental requirement within the hierarchy of needs—the need to belong. For many products, meeting this particular need is the initial step in attracting loyal customers and early adopters.

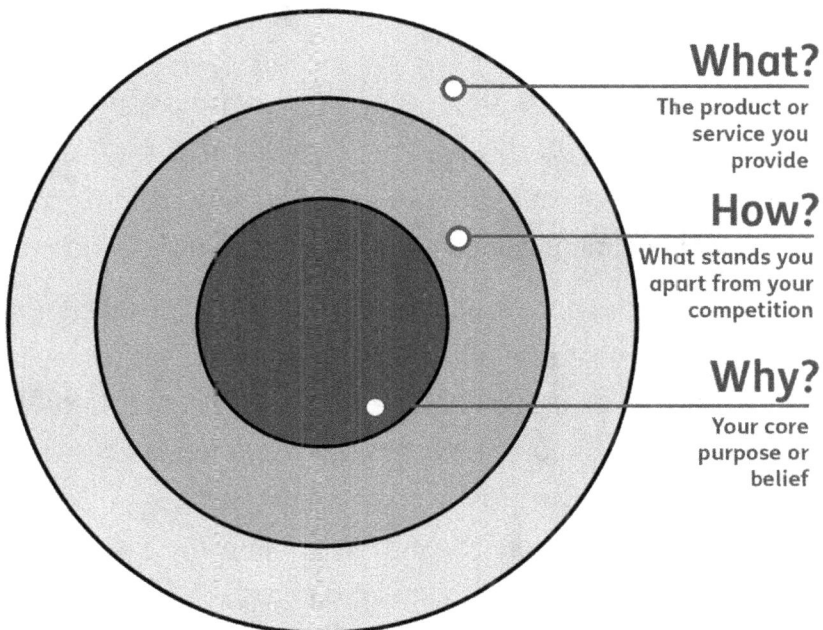

What?
The product or
service you
provide

How?
What stands you
apart from your
competition

Why?
Your core
purpose or
belief

Figure 1 Simon Sinek's Golden Circle.

With Matt's insightful perspective, we embarked on formulating a compelling "why" for our product. Matt believed that when brewers' spent grain is upcycled into flour, it directly appeals to people's desire for consuming baked goods (an obvious application with flour) like breads and desserts while still enabling a low-carb intake. On the other hand, I had reservations about the flour's ability to compete as a low-carb ingredient due to strong incumbents in the market like almond and coconut flour. Although the bakeability of spent grain was superior, I believed the incremental improvement wouldn't be significant enough to carve out a substantial market share. Instead, I urged us to adopt a forward-thinking approach, envisioning why anyone would care about this ingredient ten years down the line. My prediction was that the flour would align with corporate "green goals" and cater to the sustainability sensibilities of individual consumers. The emergence of the "ESG" (environmental, social, and governance) theme on Wall Street and the UN's recognition of food waste as a means to tackle climate change supported this perspective (https://sdgs.un.org/goals/goal12). I believed that the societal pressure to find climate solutions would provide an easier path to market penetration and funding once we officially launched.

Ultimately, we decided to focus on the low-carb market as it offered more immediate quantifiable results and a faster way to gather feedback on the flour. Our next steps were divided into two distinct paths: (a) establishing a commercial production route and scale and (b) introducing initial products to test the ingredient in the market. At that time, you may recall a company called Kodiak Cakes, which had recently gained prominence after appearing on Shark Tank. They were well on their way to becoming the dominant player in the realm of new and alternative baking mixes, available nationwide at retailers. Notably, they highlighted their higher protein content compared to regular mixes. We reasoned that a universal approach to testing would involve selecting something familiar and beloved by people, reducing the barriers to trial, and introducing the new aspect through familiarity. Thus, we decided that our first product would be a low-carb, "just add water" pancake mix, with the main ingredient, by weight, being spent grain flour. However, the trials for this product proved to be arduous and painstaking. Matt, with his amateur nutrition scientist persona, devised a matrix of desired properties for the pancake mix, encompassing factors such as fluffiness, rise, bakeability, taste, and texture. Based on these parameters, he began researching the various ingredients that would yield an excellent pancake mix It's important to note that spent grain is an intriguing ingredient because it undergoes a denaturing process during brewing. In addition to carbohydrates being removed from the barley, gluten, specifically the beta-glucan protein, also undergoes denaturation This breakdown essentially yields a flour that is almost gluten-free. Although there may be slight variations across breweries, the customary brewing process yields similar results in terms of barley composition. However, this poses a significant challenge when creating a pancake mix, as the flour cannot rise on ts own, making it particularly difficult to develop a "just add water" solution.

Around this time, Matt and were introduced to a program called Project Flourish through First Presbyterian Church in Houston. Through a seemingly serendipitous web of connections, I was able to connect with the program director and gain a rough understanding of the program's structure. Essentially, Project Flourish primarily served as an accelerator for non-profit organizations. After three to four months of mentorship, participating organizations would pitch their ideas, Shark Tank-style, to a panel of accomplished Houstonians who were also church members. The cash prize, a generous $250,000 split among the winners, was provided as grants (yes, this congregation was quite affluent). The program aimed to offer funding, mentorship, connections, and recognition to non-profits in Houston. Personally, I found the concept intriguing. As a fellow Christian, I understood the mixed reactions that arise when business and church resources intersect. It goes without saying that our venture was not a non-profit, and our ultimate goal was to deliver financial returns to our investors. Nevertheless, the program director did not discriminate regarding the types of organizations that could participate, although most were indeed non-profits. As part of the program, we were matched with a connected mentor—a person who may or may not have had direct experience in our field but possessed the ability to connect us with relevant experts. Like other accelerators, we had scheduled regular check-ins, attended courses held at the church, and had various objectives to meet along the way. Matt and I entered the process with a simple concept in mind, and initially applied to Project Flourish with a few forms and a basic economic model outlining how everything could work. Surprisingly, we were selected and matched with a mentor. After a few initial meetings with our mentor, we were encouraged to figure out the drying and initial product development within the next few months, as it was crucial to have those aspects in place before Pitch Day. These initial mentor meetings took place before August 2017, leading up to Hurricane Harvey, one of the most devastating hurricanes in Houston's history. The hurricane caused extensive damage and disruption, resulting in the program being delayed by almost six months. While this was undoubtedly devastating for the city and many of our friends, Matt and I took advantage of the additional six months to continue working diligently on solving the problems before the program officially began.

Developing the technology and use cases for commercial upcycling

As Matt tackled the challenge of creating a low-carb, "just add water" pancake mix with spent grain as the primary ingredient, my task was to find a drying and milling solution that would yield dried grains and a uniform flour. The problem is relatively straightforward—there's a granular material that retains moisture (like a sponge) and needs to have that water removed. There are several ways to remove water, and the process consists of multiple stages. To illustrate the stages, imagine a soaked sponge with pores both on the inside and outside. Some pores are easily accessible and release water with a gentle squeeze. Squeezing and wringing the sponge will reach deeper pores and release more water. However, some water remains trapped inside the sponge and requires additional effort to remove. Dehydrating spent grain (and any moisture-retaining material) operates in a similar manner, involving several stages of drying. Reducing the moisture content from 80 per cent to 40 per cent is relatively straightforward. Progressing from 40 per cent to 20 per cent becomes increasingly challenging. Finally, achieving a shelf-stable moisture content of around 7 per cent is very difficult and requires substantial energy, particularly at scale. We identified various mechanisms to address these stages. First, allowing the grain to drain, which involves enabling free water to separate from the product once it exits the brewing system. Second, employing a mechanical press, usually powered by hydraulics or electricity, to compress the grain. However, even the most efficient presses can only reduce the moisture content to about 60 per cent due to the density of barley, which restricts compression and the release of additional liquid. The most challenging step is drying the grain from 60 per cent to a shelf-stable moisture level.

While I had an engineering background, my understanding of drying was fairly rudimentary. I possessed a basic idea of the necessary components for drying something: airflow, heat, and agitation, in that order of importance (arguably). To gain a deeper understanding of the principles involved in drying food byproducts like spent grain, I delved into a wide range of resources. I immersed myself in patent applications, research reports from institutions and universities, articles, government reports, and any material related to the drying of food byproducts. Additionally, I drew upon my knowledge of the oil and gas industry to comprehend the drying processes employed for various outputs. This exploration led me down a rabbit hole, expanding my understanding of drying fundamentals across diverse industries, including pulp for paper production, raw agricultural products, municipal waste (albeit unpleasant), and more. Over the course of six to seven months of research, I uncovered a breakdown of the previously mentioned steps of airflow, heat, and agitation, which could be applied in numerous ways.

During this research period, I had to continue producing grain and turning it into flour to enable Matt to develop a comprehensive understanding of spent grain's baking properties without interruption. To facilitate this, I applied my acquired knowledge by constructing my own drying system. The first step involved reducing the free water content and targeting the easily accessible pore space within the barley kernels (recall our sponge analogy). This was the relatively straightforward part. I essentially built a wine press using hydraulic presses from a home improvement store, screened compartments, and porous bags. It's worth noting that by this point I had already returned to North Dakota due to my work at Hess, and winter was fast approaching. For basic geographical context, the further north you go, the colder it gets, with temperatures routinely dropping to the sub-20s to 40s range.

Once the grain was mechanically pressed, I needed to devise a dryer that applied the principles of airflow, heat, and agitation. I decided to start with a clothes dryer. I purchased a small model from Amazon, understanding the basic heat inputs required to calculate the efficiency of the dryer. This involved knowing the type and model of heating coils in the dryer and the approximate power required to generate the desired heat. I also considered the average cost per kilowatt-hour (kWh) and the actual costs based on the average power rates in our townhome. Additionally, the dryer possessed airflow capabilities, thanks to a small fan in the system. Similarly to a convection oven commonly found in kitchens, the fan facilitated the efficient distribution of heat across a designated area or space. Lastly, a clothes dryer spins, providing a form of agitation to the input. At this stage, experimentation was key to identifying the most impactful effects. As previously mentioned, there is an order of importance to drying, where each subsequent step is almost ineffective unless the preceding one has taken place. As the mechanical press could only achieve a certain level of moisture content (around 60 per cent) with my home system, it did not warrant further investment of time.

Addressing airflow was the first challenge. When dealing with particles like spent grain or other food byproducts, the fine particles, akin to dust, created certain issues. Firstly, there was a safety hazard since these particles tended to accumulate in certain areas and carbonize due to repeated heating and cooling from dryer use. This blackened dust could become highly flammable. This is why dryers are equipped with lint catchers or screens to prevent lint from getting trapped in dryer crevices. However, in the case of organics, they differed from lint found in clothes as they typically had higher moisture content, causing them to stick and obstruct airflow. To resolve this, I explored dust collection systems and discovered a dual benefit for the system. Essentially, airflow is the primary driver of the drying process. If there was a way to enhance airflow, such as employing a vacuum on the other side of the system to pull air, it would have a more significant impact on the input product. The second advantage was improving system safety by capturing dust and enabling its recycling back into the final output. Through preliminary research, I found that, while there were applications of this concept, none specifically pertained to food production.

The heating aspect of the drying process posed certain limitations in terms of available applications for testing at home. I had a restricted power supply before risking eviction by my housemates. Additionally, the cost of infrared or open fire systems was prohibitive at the time. Thus, I postponed this particular step for future exploration.

Agitation, on the other hand, was relatively easy to comprehend. The greater the agitation, the more effective the drying process. Consider the boiling of pasta as an analogy. While the hot water plays a vital role in soaking and cooking the pasta, there is another process that contributes to reducing boiling time. It involves the bubbles formed by the active gasification of the water during boiling. These bubbles create pockets of gas (steam) that rise through the pot, vigorously jostling and shaking the pasta. This allows for greater contact between the pasta and the hot boiling water, resulting in more efficient drying. Similarly, when agitating a drying substance, the more it is shaken and moved, the more opportunities arise for hot air to interact with a larger surface area, facilitating more effective drying. Imagine using a clothes dryer without the spinning function. Although the clothes would eventually dry, it would likely take considerably longer since each item would have varying levels of contact with the hot air generated by the system. As mentioned, we utilized a spinning clothes dryer, but I wanted to explore ways to increase agitation in the system. My first attempt involved shaking the entire dryer while it was running. I purchased a small shaker typically used for cement mixing and rigged it with a spring attached to the dryer. Needless to say, it immediately destroyed the appliance. Who knew clothes dryers weren't built to withstand violent shaking? My next attempt involved adding balls to the dryer to create more impactful jarring movements, aiming to break up the product, promote separation, and improve drying results.

Unfortunately, this approach did not yield significant measurable improvements. Although I wished to continue experimenting with shaking the system itself, I did not feel inclined to purchase another dryer. This aspect would also be set aside for future exploration.

Every time I attempted to dry the grain, it attracted attention. During winter, steam would billow out of the garage, leading to a few visits from the police. At the time, there were drug-related issues in the area, and I was repeatedly questioned as to whether I was operating a meth lab. Drying grain in a Minot, ND garage during winter was apparently an unbelievable truth, and the large plumes of steam even prompted a police visit one evening.

While refining the technology, I encountered a step that I hadn't mentioned before but would later discover after launching the business: blending. Consider the scenario of drying clothes and adding a dry towel to the dryer along with the wet clothes. A quick Google search would reveal that the presence of the dry towel speeds up the drying process. This occurs because, while the energy is used to evaporate the water from the wet clothes, the dry towel simultaneously absorbs moisture. Let's examine this concept roughly with numbers. Suppose the wet clothes have 80 per cent moisture content, while the dry towel has 0 per cent. When mixed in the dryer, the average moisture content drops proportionally to the weight of the dry towel relative to the weight of the wet clothes. So, perhaps the initial 80 per cent moisture content decreases to 60 per cent due to the dry towel. Consequently, the dryer has to work less to dry all the clothes since it is primarily influenced by the overall moisture content in the system. This principle would only become relevant later in the startup's lifecycle when we aimed to commercialize the ingredient for B2B (business-to-business) sales.

While Matt diligently worked on perfecting the pancake mix, which required over 100 trials, I began exploring turnkey solutions for our needs. This approach was inspired by my experience in the oil and gas industry. Scaling a business would entail manufacturing capabilities throughout the entire vertical, encompassing equipment, logistics, distribution, and more. Each stage involved distinct requirements in terms of expertise, supply chain access, and capital. Early on, we had to decide whether we would become an equipment manufacturer, developing our own drying technology (as some had done), a producer utilizing existing technologies to pursue various market opportunities, or simply a purchaser of the final product, such as a CPG company or bakery that solely purchases the output for use in finished goods delivered to customers.

This marked the first of many errors that would ultimately contribute to the failure of the startup. We naively attempted to pursue both technological utilization (as a producer) and market development (as a CPG business) with minimal experience, knowledge, and capital. Over the years, I've come to realize the importance of starting small, focusing on a niche, and perfecting one's craft as a proven method for disruption. However, enticed by the prospect of building a B2B firm while promoting upcycled products through a CPG channel, we set out to do both.

Eureka! Discovering the technology that would lead to the launch of our startup

To explore drying technologies that aligned with the principles I had researched and applied at home, I began sending emails to various firms mentioned in the materials I had reviewed. To my surprise, many responded. Now, it's worth noting that I still had access to my Colorado School of Mines student email address, and I presented my interest in their company from the perspective of a student pursuing a project. While my intention was genuine, I admit it may have been slightly misleading. Nonetheless, many of these companies referred me to their senior engineers, who were pleased to engage in technical discussions with another engineer. This proved to be immensely informative. I had no idea that something as seemingly straightforward as drying had advanced applications across various industries. After two months of calls and emails, I compiled a shortlist of ten potential drying technologies that could suit our needs. It was relatively straightforward to identify the companies that manufactured these machines. Many of them accepted my request to visit their facilities and witness their dryers in action. As a result, I scheduled nine meetings. However, before conducting any tests, I needed to provide them with a sample of our product. This presented a challenge. Every time I wanted to make a site visit, I had two options: drive to the nearest brewery, which involved a four-hour round trip to Bismarck, ND, or coordinate with a local brewer near the equipment supplier and arrange to pick up a batch of their grain upon my arrival in the city. While cities like Denver and Houston posed no problem, breweries became less prevalent as

I ventured further into the heartland. Additionally, each time I called a brewery to coordinate a pick-up, I had to pitch them on what I was doing, why I needed a five-gallon bucket of fresh grain, and why they should assist me. Although this process was somewhat frustrating, it served as good practice for selling and provided valuable insights. Occasionally, I would make the drive to Bismarck, and on other occasions, I was fortunate to find a local brewery. Unfortunately, none of the nine manufacturers were able to achieve satisfactory results for our business. While we came close in certain cases, the equipment was either prohibitively expensive or the drying times and complexity did not meet our requirements. By this point, it was either January or February, and we were approaching the halfway mark of Project Flourish. Matt was nearing completion of an initial product and had been hosting taste testing parties at his apartment and sending samples to family members to gather feedback directly from potential users. On the other hand, I was still far from finding a solution. During my final meeting with a manufacturer on my list, I happened to run into the engineer who had introduced me to the lead technician responsible for conducting my test at their facility. Through our conversation, he mentioned the existence of a technology that might align with our product needs. The manufacturer he referred to was located on the East Coast, and he suggested it would be worthwhile to inquire if they could assist us. Back in North Dakota, I reached out and had a general conversation with a sales engineer about our objectives. After a few weeks of back and forth, I was put in contact with their lead engineer and technical director. It seemed promising. The technology itself was straightforward, but certain configurations were needed to achieve the significant improvement we were seeking. We arranged a test using spent grain and implemented some modifications I had requested on their lab equipment. I shipped the spent grain via parcel delivery and eagerly awaited the results while traveling to Houston for another mentorship meeting. While in Houston, I received the results and was absolutely astonished. They were able to dry in minutes what conventional systems would take hours to achieve. Initially, I found it hard to believe. After some convincing, I requested to be present for a test to see the results firsthand. Consequently, I embarked on an intricately orchestrated process: packing the spent grain in dry ice in North Dakota, shipping it to the manufacturer, and timing my flight to pick it up from a nearby post office before delivering it to them for the trial. Lo and behold, the test was successful. It felt as though I had stumbled upon a hidden treasure and needed to keep it a secret.

Finally, we had our solution. Although still in the early stages of design, the core functions we needed to test the product in the real world were present. We understood how to process the ingredient, Matt had gained insights into how the product behaved in various baking applications, and together with our mentor, we were developing a business plan to be presented on pitch day.

6
Foundations

The start of my family's journey in America—1991 to 1996

Even with my dad's first paycheck, he was routinely sending money back home in order to help support his family and the efforts of war against the communists abroad. Even to this day, our family has been sending money back every month in order to continue to support the people that were left behind there. Although he wanted to keep sending money back he knew he also wanted to attend school, and continue his engineering degree. The problem was that he was making so little, that he had to prioritize whether sending money back or going to school was the wisest use of resources. So he chose the former, stopped going to school, and picked up a part-time taxi job in order to make ends meet as he sent money back. He too was working on establishing a church in Denver, and also began a fellowship of other Ethiopians and Eritreans in the Denver and Boulder area. So, at this time, my dad was working two jobs, and eventually established the church, which became known as Ethiopian Evangelical Church Denver. As the church began to take more and more of my dad's time, he was looking to meet other Ethiopian church leaders, as well as attend conferences in order to learn more about establishing the ministry in Denver. It was at this time he had a friend who was living in Canada at the time. This friend had invited my dad to come to Montreal for one of these conferences that my dad was interested in. This would be an Ethiopian gathering of various church congregations around eastern United States and eastern Canada. So my dad packed up his little tiny Toyota Celica, and drove from Denver to Montreal. This was in July 1989. Now my mom was also invited as she was in that area as well, and also made her way down to Montreal for this conference. While they were both in Montreal, my dad's friend knew of this girl that was coming down from Ottawa, who was super nice, and recommended that my dad meet her as she was also involved with a local fellowship trying to establish a church. So my dad and his friend met up with this girl, who would later one day become my mom, and some of her friends after one of the first days of the conference. At the end of that evening, my dad and my mom were infatuated with each other. My dad extended his stay in Montreal for two weeks, in order to spend more time with my mom and establish a relationship before he had to drive back to Denver. My dad would recall very fun stories of how they dated long distance for the next six months. At this time he had moved out from living in that apartment with his cousin, and was staying with some church friends, who were white, in their basement bedroom. These people have remained friends of our family ever since. While he was living there, my dad would routinely call my mom during the next six months while they were dating, using these friends' telephone. The issue though was that this was 1989, and international calls were expensive. My dad told me a story of them showing him a telephone bill after a couple months, saying that my dad needed to pony up a lot of money to repay them after making so many international calls to my mom.

The beginning of our family and the start of the long journey out of poverty

By the end of the six months my dad and mom knew they wanted to marry each other, so my dad made his way up to Ottawa, and proposed on New Year's Eve. I knew I got my romantic sense from somewhere. On August 8, 1990, my dad and mom got married in Ottawa, Canada, having a very simple wedding, and an Ethiopian celebration that evening with a few friends and family. They honeymooned at Niagara Falls and explored various beautiful cities of Canada. Due to complications of my mom's citizen status in Canada, she was not allowed to actually immigrate to the United States until her citizenship was cleared. So they painfully remained long distance until February 1991. Once she immigrated to the United States, she also got right to work at an airport gift shop, and my dad continued working at the pharmacy and driving a taxi for the next year and a half. During that time my mom became aware that my dad was clearly smart and underserving his gifts and talents doing more laborious work. So, in the fall of 1992, my dad went back to school, worked as a tutor, and continue driving a taxi part time while my mom worked various jobs to help make ends meet for the family. They had saved up enough money to buy a small townhome in Denver, as my dad wanted to quickly assume ownership of property as early as possible. During those undergraduate years, my dad also worked as a teaching assistant (TA) doing research, allowing him to eventually take some grad-level engineering courses. To bring in additional income my dad worked as a tutor in math and electronics at the Community College of Denver. During this time, there were still many Ethiopians and Eritreans in Denver that were inspired by my dad while he was tutoring them, to pursue higher education and really accomplish something greater than working a mediocre job in this country. He really inspired people to take advantage of everything the United States had to offer them. I was born in February of 1994, and my parents made the tough decision for my mom to stay at home so that I would have that type of foundation growing up.

While he had to retake quite a few courses that would not transfer from the USSR, my dad graduated with an undergraduate degree in electrical engineering in 1995. Although the job market was really tough, my dad was determined to find work as things were pretty tight at home. The TA work was great during the semester, as he was able to continue his education toward a master's degree, and get paid some income to provide assistance to his advisor and professor. Unfortunately, that summer in 1995 he was unable to find work as his specialty was in utilities, and California had already begun regulating utilities as they were coming out of the recession in 1988 and 1989. So it was difficult for a young engineer to find work in utilities, as the entire nation was paying attention to what California was doing and how the market would react to that regulatory decision. Additionally there was a high saturation of seasoned engineers that did not have work, making it virtually impossible for somebody without experience to find work. At this point, my dad was almost 30, and my brother was on the way and would be born in September of 1995. So in the fall of 1995 he continued doing TA work, attending as many job fairs as he could and working some part-time jobs on the side in order to bring some income in for the family. Fortunately, in November of that year, an organization known as Loral Space & Communications Inc was looking for programmers to bring in for some defense studies. My dad had experience coding in Fortran, and while his electrical engineering degree did not necessarily coincide with what they were looking for, they were very interested in his software background. By December of that year, my dad went in for an in-person interview, and would not hear back about the job until later in January. So in the interim, not knowing whether or not he was going to get the job, and needing to bring in even more money now that my brother was in the picture, my dad began applying for a commercial bus driving job. And I kid you not, on the first week of the bus driving job, after attending nearly three weeks of training, my dad received an offer to be a software engineer, making $33,000 a year, at Loral Space & Communications Inc in Colorado Springs, Colorado. So we moved to Colorado Springs later that spring of 1996, after my dad was able to sell the townhome that he bought with my mom, to her sister who had made it from Nairobi, Kenya to Denver, Colorado, and used the proceeds to make a down payment on a home in Colorado Springs.

7

Launch

Building and preparing for the launch of Grain4Grain—spring 2018 to fall 2018

Pitch day. The premise was simple: a board of influential church members would judge the pitches for Project Flourish throughout the day. This event primarily aimed to assist non-profits, and interestingly, I still maintain a relationship with one of the founders of Every Shelter.

To prepare, Matt, a former partner, and I crafted a concise five-minute deck outlining the market vision and technology concept, including samples of the product, to exemplify the commercial and CPG opportunity. Prior to the pitch, we focused on refining our purpose and enlisted the help of a talented graphic designer to create cohesive branding. The final step was formulating our ask. Structured as a grant, the funds would cover equipment capital expenditure and working capital to launch a pilot facility. Matt and I planned to remain employed at our respective companies while financially supporting our former partner's dedicated year of work in Houston, TX. This approach allowed us to de-risk potential financial implications and focus on perfecting the technology and product aspects while not yet working full time, free from external pressures to meet revenue targets during the R&D stage.

On the day of the pitch, we presented samples created by Matt that showcased spent grain as the main ingredient. We complemented them with a compelling nutrition fact sheet highlighting high protein content, low carbs, and low fat. While reflecting on our journey and decisions, we've come to realize that certain mistakes were not initially obvious. However, one particular mistake stands out: our decision to pre-bake all the samples ahead of time. Our rationale was to be fully prepared for the pitch and avoid any potential mishaps in cooking the product live. Ordinarily, this would have been a reasonable approach. However, due to the high fiber content of our mixes, the optimal time to consume them is immediately or within a few minutes to allow for cooling. We opted for waffles due to their consistent appearance and convenient pockets for holding toppings, which minimized potential messes during consumption. However, our decision had two major drawbacks: waffles tend to be thin and prone to quick drying, and the time gap between preparation and presentation was nearly an hour due to sound check requirements. Consequently, the samples further dried out during this period. Although we were primarily concerned about the product getting cold, we attempted to address this by purchasing a toaster oven to keep the waffles warm while our presentation took place. The unfortunate result was that the toaster oven actually accelerated the drying process, leaving me unwittingly serving cardboard-like waffles to the judges, all the while wearing a smile on my face.

As I returned to the stage for questions, which I now struggle to recall, it became apparent that no one was consuming the samples. Perhaps a couple of bites were taken, but that was all. It was when a senior executive, with extensive experience in the oil and gas industry, raised his hand to ask a question mid-bite that the dryness became glaringly evident. He coughed and subtly commented on the lack of moisture. Realizing our grave error, I muttered a few profanities under my breath, fully aware of our misstep. Shortly thereafter, we were ushered out, and the following morning, I found myself on a flight back to North Dakota. The news soon arrived that we had lost the competition. A primary reason for this outcome was the judges' concern that the product's poor quality indicated that, despite the merits of the idea itself, it had no chance of succeeding. However, as a founding group, we resolved to proceed with the purchase of the grain drier we had previously tested. We considered it a prudent move in the event that we could raise the necessary capital to launch a business based on it. Given the equipment's cost and the opportunity to acquire a refurbished unit directly from the original equipment manufacturer (OEM) at approximately 50 per cent of the price of a new unit, it seemed too good to pass up. We presented this opportunity to our other partner, but for various reasons, he was unable to move forward with the required capital investment. We mutually agreed that he would step down from any founder role and consequently reduce his theoretical stake in the future venture. However, he has remained a steadfast friend and minor shareholder throughout our entire entrepreneurial journey.

Maybe we were really on to something

Matt and I found ourselves back at square one, searching for alternative methods to test our venture while juggling our day jobs, which we had neglected during the bustling accelerator program. After a month or two had passed, we received a call from the program's head, inviting us to the award ceremony and an expo at their church, showcasing the projects that had gone through the cohort. Although it felt like a consolation "prize", we recognized the debt of gratitude we owed them and agreed to set up a booth.

This time around, we approached the event with a more relaxed mindset, as we had already accepted our defeat prior to its commencement. Consequently, the pressure to perform had dissipated, allowing us to enjoy ourselves while sharing our concept with the booth visitors and treating them to freshly made upcycled pancakes. Ironically, as we served these delectable pancakes, the judges made their rounds and sampled the fresher version. Each of them expressed a similar sentiment, along the lines of, "Wow, why didn't you serve this fresh at the event? You might have won if you had!" While this was frustrating, as it highlighted our own foolishness, it also provided some confirmation that the idea of utilizing upcycled ingredients in products was not as far-fetched as we initially believed.

Consider this: if you were someone seeking to embrace a more environmentally conscious lifestyle, the options available to you were often limited to obscure lab-developed products, consuming insects, or utilizing upcycled ingredients (albeit a simplified set of examples, the point remains). For individuals like the affluent church congregants, the conceptual model of taking something that was once discarded and giving it new purpose ("life") resonated deeply, echoing numerous religious themes, particularly in Judeo-Christian traditions. Additionally, the notion of consuming such products required minimal mental leaps in terms of safety and acceptability. Kudos to Matt for skillfully achieving this by crafting a tasty, low-carb product.

The ceremony itself proved to be a delightful occasion, as we reconnected with fellow program participants and learned more about the remarkable work they were undertaking. The cliché cardboard checks were presented, and the event concluded. Later that day, our mentor and her husband invited us to lunch, during which they extended our first investment offer. It was a straightforward proposition: $60,000 for a 10 per cent stake in the business and a board seat. Both Matt and I felt deeply honored yet taken aback. Their faith in us stemmed not only from the effort we had invested in refining the concept but also from the fact that the product genuinely pleased palates in a public setting.

Raising money for the first time and a few lessons learned on the way

Now, let me recount one of the initial mistakes I made as a founder. I treated that pre-seed capital as merely the first step toward securing additional follow-on investments, contingent upon strong future unit economics, robust top-line growth, and substantial reinvestment in advertising, marketing, and operational support. In hindsight, we should have prioritized leveraging the expertise of our mentors and establishing alignment not only regarding the exit strategy but also the initial committed path forward. Once we had secured that commitment, I seized the momentum to pursue additional capital. However, I was completely oblivious to the intricacies of fundraising. Concepts like bridge rounds, stages of raising, SAFE notes, convertibles, distinctions between venture and small or medium business style investments, and the nuances of pure startup plays were foreign to me.

As I engaged in conversations with friends and high-net-worth individuals within my network, individuals I had encountered throughout the years, I began to develop our fundraising strategy. I relied on the rudimentary framework I had learned in my entrepreneurship class during college: Angel -> Seed -> Series (A, B, C, and so forth) -> exit/IPO. The premise was that each stage would require several years to reach, with the early phases demanding substantial R&D and testing before a successful launch could be achieved. One of the most common errors I now observe when inexperienced founders raise funds is a misalignment between their roadmap and their cash flow and balance sheet management. Even if the decision is to forgo raising altogether and continue bootstrapping, not comprehending the sources of funding (e.g., pre-funded invoices, debt, or fundraising) and lacking a detailed plan for managing those finances can lead to numerous headaches and potentially catastrophic scenarios.

On our end, as we engaged with more investors, we organized roundtable discussions and discovered that people were highly enthusiastic about the concept. However, they exhibited a range of perspectives when it came to investment terms. Most of them hailed from private equity backgrounds, which, in essence, represent a distinct investment philosophy compared to early-stage investing. Let's explore some key disparities: private equity focuses on mature companies, while venture/early-stage investing centers around startups and nascent enterprises. Private equity investments are significant in scale, whereas venture/early-stage investments tend to be more modest. Private equity entails lower risk due to predictable operations, whereas venture/early-stage investments carry higher risk but the potential for substantial returns. Furthermore, private equity investments possess a longer investment horizon of five to ten years, while venture/early-stage investments aim for exits within three to seven years or potentially longer.

Another common mistake among entrepreneurs, and here I'm mainly referring to myself, is their inclination toward opportunism and unwavering optimism. While these traits are vital for fostering determination, resilience, and a willingness to learn and adapt, they also create a strong bias that is challenging to overcome. This bias often manifests as a tendency to rely heavily on our strengths while neglecting or inadequately assessing our weaknesses. This flaw became evident as we finalized the fundraising process and developed a pro forma that projected the business's performance after the injection of capital. The amount of capital and time we allocated to showcase exponential growth was, in retrospect, rather comical. Based on my anecdotal rule of thumb, early-stage manufacturing businesses typically require twice as much capital and three times as long to become operational. Now, don't misunderstand me—I've received this advice numerous times from individuals like my father and other mentors in my life. The notion of requesting more than what is immediately required and extending projected timelines aligns with the common adage of "underpromising and overdelivering". However, my unbridled optimism and Matt's and my naivety about the true challenges of this endeavor led us to perhaps our most significant error: raising an inadequate amount of funds initially. I could dwell on the terms, the early establishment of a board of directors, and other parameters, but, in retrospect, we needed those measures because we were still uncertain about the appropriate path forward. At best, this was a project that demanded substantial tough love and meticulous attention to transform it into a sustainable business. I will delve deeper into our board's role later.

Over the ensuing summer months, we diligently finalized the terms and conditions of our fundraising efforts and established the new entity. The entire process brimmed with excitement. My former manager at Hess Corporation had offered support, as much as a boss could, acknowledging my courage to venture out on my own. He understood that if I successfully completed the fundraising, I would depart from the company. I distinctly recall the moment when we secured the final signature on the operating agreement. I entered his office to share the news that we had achieved our goal and that I would be tendering my resignation within the next two weeks. In the following days, I wrapped up all my ongoing projects, packed my modest car, and embarked on the journey back to Colorado. Matt and I still hadn't secured a location and couldn't commit to an initial lease until the business entity was established and funds were procured.

During this transitional period, we also deliberated on the ideal location. Denver, Boulder, and Austin emerged as compelling choices for launching our venture. However, Matt and I had agreed, prior to the operating agreement's completion, that one of us would work full time to cover living expenses until the business generated sufficient revenue to support a salary or until the business justified securing additional funds for that purpose. We ultimately decided that Matt would assume that role since he resided in a city, while I was based in North Dakota Moreover, Matt had met his girlfriend at the time, who has now become his wife, and there were constraints preventing her relocation. Thus, due to these circumstances, we settled on San Antonio as our home for the next five years—the city where Matt was already situated for his job.

Making the move to San Antonio, TX

In hindsight, I believe this choice may have deprived Grain4Grain of potential opportunities that could have provided additional growth tools. While many speculative factors contributed to this, the main drawbacks of San Antonio, in comparison to the aforementioned cities and more, encompassed its population demographics, venture and startup landscape, and the existing business environment. Consider that we were introducing an environmentally friendly, health-conscious flour—an endeavor that may not immediately align with the notion of central Texas as an ideal launchpad. Additionally, our product commanded a premium due to its higher quality, which in turn necessitated a higher price point that could be prohibitive for lower-income consumers. Approximately one in seven San Antonians grapple with Type 2 diabetes, and nearly 30 per cent (if not more presently) are prediabetic. Moreover, San Antonio holds the unenviable distinction of being the most impoverished major metropolitan area in the United States. These factors posed numerous challenges in the years to come. San Antonio boasted a fledgling startup and venture culture. At the time, investments primarily gravitated toward cybersecurity due to the city's substantial military presence and its surrounding regions. While these circumstances presented evident obstacles in terms of fundraising and awareness, the most arduous reality lay in the isolation experienced as entrepreneurs running a startup. Communities of fellow startups and founders are profoundly underrated, in my opinion. These communities serve as lifelines during times of need and serve as fertile grounds for talent acquisition, ultimately fostering the growth of a vibrant ecosystem and an accessible talent pool as the business or project flourishes. Lastly, the existing businesses in San Antonio and the investments surrounding them predominantly revolved around real estate, agriculture, services, and industrial manufacturing. Many of these enterprises had been established long before our arrival and were relatively obscure yet sizeable companies. Correspondingly, investments in those sectors predominated, making it challenging to gain traction within the community for the nature of our work. Admittedly, these critiques largely generalize the situation, and numerous companies and startups have managed to thrive. Nevertheless, the city poses several obstacles that would likely be absent in alternative locations.

San Antonio does offer several advantages for manufacturers and food and beverage businesses. To begin, input costs are considerably lower in comparison to other potential cities we could have chosen. These costs encompass utilities, transportation, labor, materials, and third-party services, among others. Almost everything came at a slightly reduced price in this city. Moreover, there are specific benefits for food companies, considering that HEB (Texas's largest grocery chain) is headquartered there, and a burgeoning food service scene allows startups to swiftly iterate flavors and styles. San Antonio also possesses a devoted customer base for emerging businesses. Perhaps this stems from the city's nascent entrepreneurial scene. Nonetheless, for the time being, San Antonio undeniably presents exceptional advantages for early-stage startups striving to expeditiously establish their presence.

For those who have ventured into the realm of business education, whether at the undergraduate or postgraduate level, a prevailing theme when studying entrepreneurship is the notion of de-risking the founder's stake, particularly if they are committing a significant amount of time. Many lessons emphasize the importance of maintaining a burn rate that covers two to three years, encompassing the salaries of the founders and key hires. Now, we're not talking exorbitant salaries, but rather enough to allow these essential individuals to dedicate their focus and attention without the worry of where their next meal will come from. Unfortunately, Matt and I naively assumed that his part-time effort and my full-time commitment would suffice. Regrettably, this approach proved detrimental, resulting in sluggish progress during the initial stages and creating a situation ripe for conflicts concerning time versus money. I must stress that I never recommend this approach to anyone. If you're a founder, go all-in and ensure that your living expenses are funded by contributors. Refusing to pay yourself is not a demonstration of flexibility or a means to leverage future opportunities. Instead, it creates difficult scenarios that cloud judgment at crucial crossroads— a lesson I wish I could go back in time to learn. Of course, this perspective differs significantly from that of bootstrapped businesses. Nonetheless, the principle of ensuring your basic needs are met remains vital. The moment you adopt a survivalist mindset and neglect strategy and long-term thinking, it's better to halt your endeavors and close up shop.

One essential task on my agenda before relocating to San Antonio was to find a suitable location for our first pilot plant. We scoured commercial facility listings, diligently seeking a space that would align with our early-stage parameters. Essentially, we sought a location that offered the cost advantages of a small square footage, provided the necessary power input to operate our acquired unit, and could be retrofitted for food safety at a reasonable expense. Surprisingly, this proved to be a daunting challenge. Remember, we hadn't raised a substantial amount of money. Consequently, certain barriers, some necessary and others not, hindered our options for the initial pilot location. Setting a radius of 50 miles from the city center of San Antonio, we discovered a grand total of two potential sites. While I remained in Colorado, Matt personally visited a couple of these locations, embarking on tours arranged by an online broker. The first site we encountered had the potential to work, but the extensive retrofitting and upgrades required to ensure food safety proved cost-prohibitive, eroding nearly 40 per cent of our initial capital outlay. Some of the necessary upgrades involved securing an adequate power supply to operate our first test unit. Our innovation at the time demanded significant electricity availability, as opposed to our subsequent iteration that leveraged natural gas—a far more cost-effective alternative. The second location we stumbled upon appeared rather peculiar at first glance, but it met our requirements. Admittedly, this site seemed incongruous considering that we were creating an environmentally friendly flour and CPGs, which would utilize said flour and be sold to customers. The location itself was an old chandelier satellite facility boasting the necessary power due to the extensive lighting requirements of a showroom. Additionally, it was situated in a commercial area in a different county, just beyond our initial expectations. Nestled within an old lumber yard, it offered grandfathered-in permitting and regulatory benefits that would have entailed a six-month delay had we opted for a site closer to the city center. I flew down from Colorado to meet up with Matt and our realtor, reviewing the site plan, outlining the facility construction process, and subsequently engaging in negotiations regarding pricing and other tenant improvements essential to commence our startup operations. Once the funds from our initial investors materialized, and all the legal formalities were in order, we proceeded to finalize lease negotiations, marking the start of my preparations to relocate to San Antonio.

During this period, Matt resided with a coworker in a cramped two-bedroom apartment. Countless adventures unfolded within those walls. As for me, I settled for the family room, sleeping on a mattress placed directly on the floor. This arrangement persisted for the next two months until we purchased our first house in San Antonio. As I mentioned earlier, the location we secured necessitated retrofitting and construction efforts to ensure it met the requirements for food manufacturing. With limited funding available to hire contractors for all aspects of the work, I had to roll up my sleeves and take on some of the tasks myself. We did engage contractors to establish a loading dock area, erect separating walls within our leased space, and handle the permitted work, such as electrical and plumbing. However, I found myself drawing upon my experiences as a high schooler, assisting my father in upgrading old rental homes, to tackle the remaining tasks. The list of work required to pass a health inspection was extensive, encompassing floor, ceiling, and wall renovations, substantial repainting, various installations (including sinks and equipment), and ventilation adjustments. I managed to accomplish all of these tasks with the assistance of Matt, who proved invaluable. While I devoted most of my time to preparing the plant for our initial production, Matt focused on getting our first product ready for demos and any markets we could penetrate. By serendipity, we discovered that one of the nation's most prestigious farmers markets was held in San Antonio, specifically in an area called the Pearl. However, gaining entry required our plant to be fully operational for a tour. In the meantime, as we readied the facility, Matt and I narrowed down our initial product offerings, opting to proceed with our original pancake and waffle mix—the very product we pitched at the Project Flourish pitch day. We believed this product would serve as an excellent introduction for families and health enthusiasts seeking to incorporate sustainable options into their diets. We retained the same recipe, ensuring the mix remained a simple "just add water" solution. Additionally, during our strategic deliberations, we recognized the opportunity to introduce a second product simultaneously—the flour itself, which we produced as a primary ingredient. Considering the long-term vision of establishing a substantial B2B business, we concluded that launching both Stock keeping units simultaneously would work in our best interest. Moving forward, our objective was to secure a name for our startup and our first two products.

Choosing our name and gearing up for the launch of our business

There is a great deal of importance in choosing the initial name for your business. Reflecting on my first attempt in this venture, I now realize the advantages of an ambiguous and concise name (one or two syllables, at most) that allows for brand power and flexibility in offerings. However, there is also merit in naming your business according to its specific purpose. For instance, if you specialize in pool repair, it is best to name your business as "[City's Name] Best Pool Repair", considering both SEO (search engine optimization) strategy and recognition. However, in cases where offerings may evolve or when the brand's vision remains unknown, it can be beneficial to have a slightly ambiguous name to begin with. While raising money in the spring of that year, I visited my family and embarked on a quick weekend ski trip. As I drove back with a friend, I recognized the immense joy I derived from being in the mountains and contemplated the potential of our venture in evoking that feeling among people who appreciate the outdoors and its preservation. Additionally, my growing interest in backcountry skiing inspired me with the idea of transforming something relatively unknown, like the backcountry or wilderness, into a tangible product, much like a "mill" does for flour. Consequently, the original parent name for our business became Backcountry Mills. However, as we iterated on the website and initial packaging designs, we found that the name felt overly long and somewhat challenging to work with. Although I personally liked the name and saw its potential, Matt believed we needed a name that better represented our product, facilitating a quicker connection with customers looking to make purchases at markets, stores, or online. So, we returned to the drawing board multiple times in search of a suitable name.

Matt and I both held great respect for businesses that incorporated philanthropy into their operations. I admired companies like Warby Parker or Toms, which donated a portion of their products to people in need as customers made purchases. Naturally, we were aware of the potential pitfalls associated with such philanthropic models, but in theory they could be tailored effectively to our local community. There are various iterations of this concept, whether through product-based donations or giving a portion of profits. Both Matt and I loved the idea and wanted to incorporate it into our business model. Thus, we settled on the concept of "Grain 4 Grain", wherein we would give a portion of the flour we produced back to the community through partnerships with local food banks. The idea was that, while we might not generate substantial revenue right from the start, we could at least provide a valuable ingredient that would otherwise be cost-prohibitive for our local community in San Antonio. As I mentioned earlier, the community faced a highly detrimental health crisis largely resulting from dietary preferences. We pondered the question,

"What if we could create products that the community loves, utilizing a flour that is arguably better in every nutritional aspect compared to what is typically consumed, while also incorporating educational components related to the environment and technology?" Later on, as will describe in better detail, we were able to execute that vision in a variety of ways through different events throughout the city, and it proved to be incredibly rewarding. Consequently when it came to choosing a name, we wondered if we could brand the product with the philanthropic concept front and center. In hindsight, this name may not have been the best choice but to our credit, we made the most of it and still achieved significant traction. After a few meetings and separate branding sessions where we both contemplated potential names, we settled on "Grain4Grain" as the startup name for this venture. Additionally, we sought to find a better name for the flour itself. In an earlier chapter, I mentioned that people had previously referred to this product as "spent grain" However, the term "spent grain" inherently carries connotations of waste, seconds, or leftovers. We wanted to ensure that people knew this was a premium product but took a unique path. Matt, known for his skill in alliteration and unique wordplay, approached me one night as he worked on the pancake mix. I had just returned late to the apartment after working on the facility, and he asked, "What do you think about the name 'Barely Barley'?" The idea behind it was that we were still using barley, but it was barely recognizable, indicating a significant transformation. It was a far better name than "spent grain" as it sounded more playful and approachable. After contemplating it for an evening, we both agreed it was probably the best name to move forward with, considering that we were essentially the only players in the market producing this product at the scale we proposed. And who knows, if we achieved great success, there might have been branding and licensing opportunities down the road, offering additional risk-free revenue. Next, we focused on finding a name for our pancake mix. Some of the obvious contenders in the space had already solidified the idea of high protein in consumers' minds. Companies like Kodiak Cakes, Quest Nutrition, and others dominated the high-protein subcategory for pancake mix. Additionally, the alternative ingredients space within the mix category was becoming increasingly crowded, with newcomers like Simple Mills securing significant shelf space due to substantial venture capital support. Therefore, we decided to highlight both the low-carb nature of our product and its upcycled or renewable purpose. Again, considering naming and packaging design, various routes can be taken. One option is to follow the RX Bar route, prominently displaying ingredients or nutrition facts on the front. Alternatively, a more vibrant and comprehensive branding approach can be adopted. In our case, we opted for a route similar to RX Bar, where we placed the protein, carb, and fiber content where the product name would typically be. Although I disagreed with this decision, we minimized the branding due to our lack of brand recognition at the time. It's a classic chicken-and-egg problem. How can you gain brand recognition? Likely by promoting your brand. But how can anyone recognize your brand until they know the service or product you offer? Hence, we agreed to have the brand present on the front of the package, albeit small compared to other features. After a few more weeks of iterating on the package design and website landing page, we felt that we had made sufficient progress to begin preparing for a launch. The facility was also nearing completion, and I was preparing to conduct the first trials on the equipment while Matt began working on additional products that could be part of our product roadmap utilizing spent grain. Lastly, with the assistance of Matt's fiancée (now wife), we started creating recipes for the standalone flour product.

Once we had everything in place, I reached out to the Pearl Farmers Market to initiate the process of becoming a vendor. Upon submitting our application, I realized the tremendous potential of our idea. To my surprise, the president of the market personally reached out, expressing her intrigue about our application and the company we were creating. She wanted to visit our plant and meet us. Initially, I assumed this was a routine practice, but as our business progressed, I recognized that our venture was unique and appealed to a broad audience due to its creativity, effective environmental solutions, and the production of healthy, delicious products. We arranged a meeting at the pilot plant where I demonstrated our production process and showcased the mixes we had finalized, as we worked through our product roadmap. To my delight, she approved our application on the spot. She even gave us a start date for the weekend after Thanksgiving, granting us three weeks to prepare sufficient inventory for the farmers market.

During the preparation phase, I wanted to gain firsthand experience in sampling our mixes and showcasing the possibilities with our flour. Consequently, I reached out to gyms, yoga studios, and barre studios—essentially anywhere that would welcome us and allow us to serve our products. The experience of directly serving our products to people and observing their reactions as they consumed them was absolutely invaluable. There's nothing quite like receiving immediate feedback as someone tries a food product right before your eyes. Through these interactions, we made future iterations based on customer preferences and what resonated most with them. After a few rounds of sampling, we assembled our pop-up kit, which we would use at the farmers market to prepare fresh pancakes on the spot and serve them to customers. The weekend before our official launch, we decided to kick off our website, ironing out any kinks and ensuring that people had a reliable platform to learn more about us and even purchase our products online. We both returned to our respective destinations for the Thanksgiving holiday, only to come back and fully prepare for our first weekend at the farmers market.

8

The American dream

Following the journey of how my parents went from barely making ends meet to becoming successful entrepreneurs and highly contributing members of their communities—1996 to present

Buying their first home was a very big turning point for them, but even more so when they purchased their house in Colorado Springs. At this point my dad began to read into real estate investing and had his eyes on working toward acquiring properties, turning them into rentals, and then eventually flipping them for sale or pulling cash out through refinancing. During that first year at Loral Space & Communications Inc, through pressures from the federal government during both the Bush and Clinton administrations, Lockheed merged with a portion of Martin Marietta, as the rest of the defense industry was consolidating.

As a part of this consolidation, Loral Space & Communications Inc specialized in defense, missile, and satellite work, and was absorbed by the newly formed Lockheed Martin within my dad's first year working there. This began my dad's start at Lockheed Martin, where he would end up staying for the remainder of his professional career. He dared to move around a lot within the organization and even took a brief stint outside of Lockheed in a telecom technology business. However, he would end up returning to Lockheed within a month of this stint as he was more interested in the highly technical and contributive efforts toward our national defense programs at Lockheed Martin. At this point, my dad had a new opportunity arising in an area near Littleton, CO, about an hour and a half north of Colorado Springs. So my dad wanted to utilize the home in Colorado Springs as their first rental property, and purchase a home in the new city, and begin building wealth. My parents were well aware that they were starting nearly ten years later than some of my dad's peers, and still had aspirations of retiring by 55. The only way to make that happen was either to hit it rich on the lottery, or strategically invest while living well below our means, in efforts to acquire wealth-generating assets. However, there was a hiccup with that home in Littleton, which shows a huge testament to the effort my parents made in their early days. As a part of the arrangement to keep the home in Colorado Springs, they needed a larger down payment than they had available in cash. My mom decided in order for them to keep that home in Colorado Springs, the only way for them to earn enough money for this new down payment was that she would need to work the graveyard shifts at Walmart and would do weekends at IHOP. Over the next nine months through that effort, and living very frugally, they were able to put together the $20,000 required for the down payment. They finally, in the spring of 2001, purchased their second home and were able to put their first other home in Colorado Springs up for rent. Over the next five years, I remember fairly vividly that our family did its best to make sure we felt like we had everything we needed, but definitely, we were living frugally in order to make the cash that they were assuming from the rent be available for their next investment. I remember so many times shopping at Goodwill for all of my school clothes, which to be frank I think I would do even if I was wealthy because, let's be honest, kids grow so fast that spending the same amount of money as you would for adult-size clothing on kids' clothing seems incredibly wasteful. But I digress.

My parents' exploration of business

In 2002, my dad wanted to venture into a business that would allow for them to bring in more income, and acquire more properties down the road. He knew that his earnings at Lockheed, while good, were not nearly enough to be able to bring in enough cash flow to take on the additional risk of more real estate. With the mind toward that future potential of investing, and looking for something that my mom could also work on while we kids, including my sister who was born in 2000, were out of the house. My parents also brought on a business partner, in order to make the initial purchase of the business less risky on the cash balance they had. So, with the additional flexibilities of not having to work on the weekends, and also being able to have flexibility in the evenings, they landed on a dry cleaners. The dry cleaning industry in Denver was largely, and is still largely, run by Korean immigrants. So my parents felt like they would be able to operate a dry cleaners and bring in a different flavor to the business profile, and also look for strategic placement, mostly in heavily dense city areas like the center of downtown Denver and other parts near the capital. They purchased their first cleaners with an SBA loan for $70,000 plus an additional $90,000 for new equipment and renovations. They signed a five-year lease and got right to work. Within a few months they were open, and at the height of the business, each partner was taking home about $3,000 a month and free cash flows. After five years they decided to sell the business. During this time they also sold the home in Colorado Springs, as it was difficult to be able to maintain the home themselves with it being in another town, and my dad still having a full-time job, and my mom running the cleaners. Over the five years, they accumulated the rental cash, as well as the sales purchase, and went on to purchase two townhomes just north of them near Denver in 2005. In 2007, they were able to sell the dry cleaners for close to $200,000 net, and with an additional $100,000 of cash, and a financial crisis ensuing, my dad put that cash to work immediately. Participating in state auctions for foreclosed and distressed properties, my dad within five months, tons of borrowing later, purchased close to 11 homes in five months. This was the beginning of a long decade, of fixing homes, renting them out, refinancing when the market was right, utilizing that cash to buy another home, and rinsing and repeating the process. In the early days, we could not afford technicians to work on the homes, as they would eat in the early profits required to be able to strategically refinance the homes within a short period of time. I remember spending many weekends when I did not have sports, or a test to study for, or a church program, working with my dad on all the townhomes. Whether it was putting carpet, drywall, tile, appliances up, anything and everything, we did it. It was not easy, and it required tons of work. But that strategy of working closely with the lenders eventually allowed my parents to amass a very significant portfolio of homes, which allowed them to begin looking toward not only a retirement but also other potential futures that otherwise would not have ever been imaginable just a few short years ago. While I was not necessarily around to experience a lot of the windfall that came later on, I was and am incredibly proud of my parents as I was able to watch from afar the fruits of their labor really take hold. However, the story does not necessarily stop there. In 2013, after my brother and I both went off to college, there were two spare bedrooms in their home in Littleton. My mom, who is always an enterprising human, wanted to find ways to create cash flow from the spare bedrooms. She caught wind of a Medicaid program where you would be able to work with an agency to house people with intellectual disabilities in your home. The level of income was determined based on the severity of need and dependency for those individuals. After starting with one person, and then going to two, both my dad and mom realized that there could be a business opportunity in this space.

The making of my parents' next venture

After a few years of having two young women at their home, they decided the best way was to actually create an agency that dealt directly with Medicaid and then would place people with intellectual disabilities in homes. With a heart toward empowering the Ethiopian and Eritrean communities, my parents went out to start an agency and looked to finding Ethiopians and Eritreans that were struggling, and could use the additional income. After a couple of years of research, training, and licensures, they launched an agency to do just that. By 2022, just three years into starting their agency, they were bringing in close to seven figures a year in annual income, with very appealing net margins. As I write this now, my parents are looking to expand their agency into providing other services to people with intellectual disabilities, and I'm excited to see where they take it. My dad was able to comfortably retire in his mid-50s, is enjoying running the two businesses with my mom, and is now attending seminary full time, as his long desire to teach is now seemingly possible. My parents have always long held that the community is in need of people with resources to give back not only with tangible resources but also with intangibles. This includes counseling, mentoring, tutoring, teaching, and anything else that impacts the minds and hearts of the community that they deeply love. As American as my parents are, they are also fully Ethiopian and Eritrean. Everything that they've done has been to honor their faith, and also honor their community. Very few people have been able to show such steady discipline and steadfastness as my parents. After starting in his working career in his early 30s, and my mom making the willing sacrifice to stay at home in order to give my brother, sister, and I a great home life, they have been able to, in all sense of the term, achieve the American dream. For them, the American dream was never necessarily about money, but more so about being able to be high contributors to their community, society at a local level, and nationally. If they're remembered for anything, they should be remembered as being faithful Christians, contributing citizens, wonderful parents, and loving community members. Who knows where they're going to take their businesses next, but knowing them, I won't be surprised if they start doing something totally different in the next few years.

A few lessons from my parents worth noting

While there are many learnings to be had from their lives, and the paths they chose in this country, some reflections I've made while writing this book are as follows. Living through principle and integrity is more important than we ever give credit to in this country. You hear it all the time, but when push comes to shove, living with principles and a high sense of integrity is the key to living a purposeful life. Living with a sense of urgency and frugality allows for delayed gratification to be more sustainable. Creating an intense deadline for yourself and living well below your means as common practice in the household allows for opportunities in the present term that can compound in the future. My parents' constant willingness to not assume pleasures, buy toys, and other truly unnecessary purchases meant they were not distracted from their focus on growing their accumulation of wealth-generating assets. Heck, bad habits are hardwired into me. While I think it's good to enjoy things from time to time, my parents emphasized experiential expenditures rather than material possessions. We went on vacations, rather than buying new cars, or expensive clothes. My dad, on average, drove a car for 12 years before even considering buying a "new" used car. Even now, my dad still drives around, as one of their real estate business vehicles, a 2001 Toyota Sienna minivan. While his personal car is pretty sweet, I always ask my dad, "Why don't you get a truck for the properties?" He smiles at me, and will gently reply, "Why should I, I'm driving this car for free. You never get opportunities to use something for free, so why should I stop?" My parents constantly will look for deals, always making mention that they are not looking to make other people rich, and that there is always a deal to be made, you just have to look and ask hard enough. My parents, because their path coming into the United States was so distressed, always felt like someone was out to get them. While this is not necessarily the healthiest mindset, that frame of mind for businesses has only benefited them rather than hurting them. My parents routinely would tell me, and it was true, that no one would ever care about you more than yourself, and more than God. That said, my parents also understood the value of good service. Whenever we found a service provider, or technician, or partner, that went out of their way to give us the best service, we always returned the favor, insisting on paying full price, and insisting on partnering in the future. This principled approach allowed them to have reliable services in the future that allowed them to continue to grow their businesses without many headaches as to who or where they would get help from. My last bit of reflection is a comment on their patience. My parents always played the long game. They understood that success, and wealth, and opportunities are very difficult to come by, especially for people that look like them, and at the time when they first got here. But they knew that if they were able to never lose their shirt (by which I mean lose everything), and take healthy and regular risks, eventually, overtime, they would be rewarded. Patience is a virtue and a fruit that requires a lot of cultivation and watering. It requires a strong vision for what you want, and the willingness to sacrifice current pleasures for the achievement of that vision. I don't think my parents ever knew that they were going to have a business working alongside Medicaid, but they always knew that there were going to be more and more opportunities in the future for such businesses if they stayed the course. And I think if there is a lesson that they would want all the readers of this book to walk away with, that lesson would be to be patient, and not feel the pressure and urgency of all the flaunted extravagance around us every single day. They would tell you to stay the course, have strong convictions toward the vision you have, and be willing to forego current pleasures in order to have that attained value in the future. They would tell you to still have fun, go on a vacation every now and then, and don't be afraid to go out and eat every once in a while. But they would tell you to not buy that new car, or buy the new shoes that you really don't need, or that new leather handbag that just came out from your favorite designer. Focus on the things that add value, and be patient to see it through.

9

I hate to blame Covid, but it really did mess things up

How Covid broke our momentum and forced us to make the decision of leaving this business behind or pivoting—fall 2018 to winter 2020

The farmers market was an interesting time for us. We had our spot for both Saturday and Sunday, rain or shine, every weekend. Now, most people, when promoting a CPG product at a farmers market, would generally have their stuff prepared. For example, say you are a granola manufacturer, you can just serve your granolas in little cups at the farmers market and just talk to potential customers as you go about the day. Because of the nature of what we decided was our first product, a pancake mix, we had to make it fresh on-site, including serving it with toppings like syrup. This was very annoying when operating a pop-up setup, like the one that we had, because it required a full prep of your griddle and your ingredients, as well as a washing station (which was mandated by law). So whether it was the farmers market or other pop-up opportunities, every time was essentially the same: wake up early, check what orders need to go out and other normal course of business stuff, then get out to the location 30 minutes to an hour ahead of time, prep the station, begin prepping the mix, and then hope people come out to talk to you. What made these days excruciating was that all in, every day, required close to eight hours including prep and tear down. At the beginning of our time at the farmers market, this was very valuable for us because it gave us the opportunity, as mentioned earlier, for face-to-face interactions as people were trying our product and giving us feedback on our messaging. There were many times as we were going through this startup journey that we really relied on the feedback of others to help refine whatever it is we were looking to do. Originally, we really thought we needed a tagline. An example of one of our earliest taglines was "FIGHT THE CARBS, FEED THE HUNGRY". In the early days, this was a decent tagline for getting customers to come and talk to us. But what we realized was that the name of the business, Grain4Grain, and any tagline we had, would be a mouthful. So after a few iterations of various taglines, we decided to drop taglines altogether. The benefit of doing pop-ups the way we luckily did ours was that the places and people we met were very loyal. They would frequently revisit our booth, whether it was at the farmers market or a local gym we frequented and promoted our products at. This gave us great validation of some of the facts we had with our product pipeline and would also lend well to how we pitched our story to grocery stores down the road.

Speaking of grocery stores, let me tell you about HEB.

HEB giving us an early shot

If there was ever a cult that was so widely accepted in Texas, very few things would ever rival customers' love and loyalty for HEB grocery stores. It's difficult for me to explain just how beloved HEB is in Texas unless you've experienced it yourself. Being only located in Texas and Mexico, HEB is known for tailoring their business and marketing, hard and heavy, to their region. This has rewarded them well over the last several decades. HEB has a very popular program, which as of 2018 was only five years old, called "Quest for Texas Best", or more commonly referred to as "Quest". Essentially, this is an open call for all Texas, and anybody that wants to have a presence in Texas, to pitch their best and most innovative products for consumers to the buyers and senior leadership at HEB. Now, a few weeks into operating pop-ups and our online store, I began to see that our next iteration for the business was to pursue bricks and mortar. This is because the difficulty of scaling online, and through various pop-ups, was nearly impossible without any capital at hand. Unfortunately, I couldn't accomplish or figure out any ways forward beyond just continuing to build brand awareness locally. This paid off.

What Matt and I had, which a lot of other CPG companies as well as vendors at the farmers market did not have, was an innovative story about sustainability. Don't get me wrong, there are many stories of sustainable farming practices that end up lifting local stories; but nothing brought as much technology, as well as the unique opportunity for storytelling, for a city like San Antonio, as we did. Our first of many news articles written about us was done by the *San Antonio Express*. Published on January 4, 2019, a story was written about the innovation that Matt and I were attempting to bring to the city and food production in general. To our surprise, in the beginning of a highly serendipitous year, a very faithful and loyal reader of the *San Antonio Express* news was a vice president for HEB, in charge of global sourcing. Now I won't get into who this was, or what they specifically did for HEB, but just know that he is very important to the organization. A week after it was published, I was manning the pancake griddle, and Matt and his now fiancé were manning the point of sale for our products, when a young lady approached us and began asking us about our story. Like all other times, we just shared our passion for what we were doing, shared about the products, and offered a sample. After a seemingly innocuous conversation, the young lady reached into her pocket, handed Matt a card, and said, "Reach out to me when you guys get a chance". I will never forget Matt's eyes when he read the card, how big they grew. And when he looked at me, if I hadn't known better I would have guessed he had just won $1,000,000 on the spot. He quickly handed me the card, I looked down, and there it was—a buyer from HEB. In the grocery business, think of the buyer as the gatekeeper between you and getting on shelves. They are responsible for the products they bring in and how those products perform in their respective arena. This specific buyer was from the baking aisle, home to olive oil, bacon, and other specialty baking items, which we initially would later fit into. The rest of the day flew by, with us on a high that some random newspaper article got us in front of a buyer within a week. We got home, and quickly drafted an email, which I swear we probably edited and retyped 20 times. We sent the email out and stared at our inboxes for the next few days. Obviously, I'm exaggerating, but it sure as heck felt like that.

The buyer ended up responding pretty quickly, and asked some more questions about what we were doing, and if they and a few others from their team could come up and visit our facility, and see what we were doing. We happily obliged, and quickly drove up to the pilot facility to begin the longest deep clean of my life. During their visit, which also involved the vice president that I mentioned earlier, they told me about how they heard about us from the paper, and would like for us to apply to Quest. The next steps for the application would be filling out their online form, and then paying a visit to their corporate office for them to come and see what we had to offer. So Matt and I did what we do best, prepped our sampling kit, made a fresh batch of mix, and headed to the HEB headquarters in downtown San Antonio. There we sampled for them our pancake mix as well as, I believe, keto cookies made with our flour. They loved it, and told us we would hear back about our place in the competition later in the spring. So Matt and I continued doing what we were doing, for the rest of the spring, as we waited patiently for the announcement of whether or not we had made it to the final pitch day later in August

Initial cracks forming between Matt and I

I wish I could write that we had a great time that spring, made headway in our marketing efforts, developed new products, and just flat out made a lot more money. The opposite couldn't be more true. This was probably one of the first real distinctly hard moments in Matt's and my business relationship and friendship, and the impact of that on the business. At this point, Matt had already been married and he, his wife, and I, we're all living in the same house but in separate wings of the home. This is a terrible idea. I highly do not recommend doing that, ever. What began as a pretty fun, and relatively harmless, blending of various aspects of our friendship and relationship quickly began to complicate and gray some areas that should have remained distinctly black and white. The home, which was originally purchased to act as a place where we could do work and live, quickly became a place of contention, as we were also living out our adult lives. In this span of three to four months, Matt and I argued and fought over little things that inevitably led to big decisions. While I believe as business partners we brought a good balance to each other, I don't think we were ever made to live in the same house and work together the way we did. Additionally, a big lesson learned was that, whenever you are starting a business, it is vital to have very distinct roles, and abandon as quickly as possible the mindset of everybody needs to be able to do everything. The reason being is that each person, assuming they understand their strengths and weaknesses, really need to have things that they're held accountable to. Because I was the only full-time person, that naturally led for me to do most, if not everything, or at least it felt like that. Whereas Matt was contributing a lot of capital, which inevitably created a terrible dynamic as co-founders. During this hard time, there was a lot of self reflection and realization. As commonly referenced in various forms of literature, you really don't know what you're made of until you walk through a fire. I realized many of my inadequacies and shortcomings in areas where I thought I was a great person or leader. For example, while I did understand the basics of finance and financial management, I was terrible at organizing and preparing that information for clear communication to our stakeholders, something that Matt was great at. As the spring wore on, it was evident that Matt was not really wanting to pursue this business anymore. Matt is somebody that takes great pride in his work. As is frequently the case for all of us, that pride in our work manifests itself in us believing the quality should inevitably yield the value we prescribe it. Matt suffered a classic case of "if we build it they will come" syndrome. Matt felt that the lack of immediate virality and uptake of our product was proof that the product was not the right product for the market at the time. I felt fairly differently, and that a combination of factors were bringing obstacles that were preventing us from actually making a better assessment of whether or not this product would have been a winner or not. Because of our limited capital, and the city we were in, the footprint for awareness of what we were doing was very limited to San Antonio, and sparse communications online. While Matt would eventually be correct, that the business and what we were doing was likely going to fail, I believe that his risk adverseness biased him more than he would give credit to at the time. This led to a near falling out in our friendship and almost closure of our business, before we even had a chance to hear back from HEB. Many other things also contributed to the tension between us. The lack of progress was also weighing on me, and my compulsion for work addiction led me to become an absolute pain in the ass. I know for a fact I would not have wanted to work with me in 2019. Boy, have I grown up since then.

Because of the nature of the sacrifices I made to come to San Antonio to launch the business, I carried a sense of entitlement that just made things more difficult than they had to be. It wasn't until I actually made friends and found a church that I began to improve personality-wise and, in all fairness, mental health-wise too. There are many things I would wish to take back, but I have been fortunate to learn from a lot of my mistakes during this period. And while HEB did eventually get back to us, that we were one of 20 selected finalists to come to Houston and pitch to a group of store leaders, out of hundreds of applicants—the damage was already done. To Matt's credit, he stuck around for another year, allowing us to make it through both the pitch and a very hard Covid transition.

HEB Quest for Texas Best competition

HEB had offered us the opportunity to pitch whatever products we had ready for the competition. The process was similar to other CPG pitches that you would normally see in the course of business. Go in with our products, give them a demo, and provide pricing, as well as whatever supported advertising programs you would like. These range from what we do in-house with social media and other pop-ups to promote the traffic through HEB stores, as well as coupons and other programs that we would do at HEB. The buyer we were working with showed us a couple of opportunities that would be available to us that we could lend to the pitch when the day came, to show both our readiness for the product as well as how we could look to partner with HEB in the future. But at the end of the day the pitch really predicated on the story of what we were trying to tell. The story that Matt and I had worked hard to cultivate up to that point. Which, if you remember from previous chapters, really circled around the idea of taking byproducts that were deemed lost, giving them new life, and sharing that now surplus with the community with innovative procucts, all underpinned by our technology. However, that story hadn't really been put together yet. So, with the help of an advisor as well as some friends in the startup community, we formulated a pitch that was just a simple to-the-point story about what products we were making and offering HEB customers. After a couple iterations of this pitch deck, and along with our products we were offering, our original pancake mix and the pure spent grain flour, as well as a product road map, our HEB buyer approved what we had, which allowed us to move forward to pitch day coming up later that summer in Houston, Texas.

We learned our esson about preparing the products prior to the actual pitch. So Matt and I needed to figure out exactly what we were going to serve the judges while we were pitching and having our time during Q&A. The actual pitch day was just one day in a week-long set of programming hosted by HEB. Ranging from successful companies that have been vending at HEB for a variety of time periods, to store managers that are responsible for merchandising products daily, to different third parties ranging from financial advisors to supply chain experts, and more. This is one of my first real behind-the-scene moments of understanding just how food and beverage really operates. I was able to speak and network with at least 20 different business owners ranging from a variety of different product lines all around the US that have been selling at HEB. Heck, the story is coming up, but we even found a co-packing partner as well as a new supplier during the networking periods we had in between the various programs. Now, pitch day was pretty straightforward, as you would imagine. You are pitching in front of leaders for the store, ranging from corporate to in-store partners. You give them your spiel, let them try their food, answer some questions, and wait for results. But, I have to say, of all the pitches I've given, this one was by far the most fun. HEB really made a point about having the best experience for their judges, requiring each business to make a creative effort to share who they are and the products they offer. So for us that meant we had the ability to provide up to three items for them to taste, all made fresh if possible, with the help of actual trained chefs that HEB lent us just for the pitch day. How freaking cool is that? Matt and I had already been testing a variety of recipes made with spent grain flour. So we decided to provide them a simple three-course meal made exclusively to promote the various features of spent grain flour. We decided to start with these appetizer chicken and barbacoa street tacos, using our flour for the tortilla. The main course was our pancake mix. And last was a raspberry lemon keto cake using the flour as the base of the cake, as well as a little bit of the flour in the Greek yogurt icing. The actual prep scene could have been pulled out of a TV show like The Bear from FX. It was structured that all the companies used the same commercial kitchen, with different stations, but staggered with four companies prepping at a time. I kid you not, a kimchi company literally started a fire in the kitchen. Many people were yelling and screaming and cursing at each other ... including us. Things were being thrown, food all over the ground, and something breaking every few minutes. Maybe in another life, I could have been a chef, or more likely a line cook if we are being honest. Through the chaos, and after several iterations on-site, we were able to finalize our three-course meal and have enough cake for all audience members to give them as good of an experience as we pitched as possible. I don't really remember the actual pitch, but I do remember the reaction was varied on the first two products we brought out, the tacos and pancakes. But the reception on the cake was phenomenal. Even some of the chief executives of the company pulled Matt and I aside, handing us their business cards saying "Great job" and "Love the concept". The rest of the day was pretty relaxing, with me and Matt as well as the friends that came and supported us, as well as some of our investors, most of whom lived in Texas, eating out that night and celebrating our journey to that point.

The next morning we all gathered at the conference center where the pitches were initially held, in order to find out who the winners were going to be. Now each of the 20 finalists was all but guaranteed a shelf spot by just making it to the pitch day. So, at the end of the day, everybody won something. However, cash prizes were only given to the top four teams. The cash prizes in order were $10,000, $15,000, $20,000, and $25,000. Coming into the day both Matt and I did not think we were going to win a prize at all. Honestly, we were just happy to be there and have made it that far. As they began announcing the winners they started with the last cash prize and worked their way up to the top cash prize. And to our surprise, we were one of the winners of the $10,000 cash prize as well as another team! Later that afternoon we chatted with the buyers after spending most of the day listening to the rest of the announcements on the other cash prizes and celebrating with the winners. They notified us that they were going to push to have us in stores by the end of the fall, which at the time was in two months! We celebrated throughout the evening, at a HEB-hosted after party. That night even more buyers came and approached us, asking for other products in our product road map that we had hinted at during our pitch. One buyer from the frozen aisle asked us for frozen keto waffles and pancakes, another asked us for frozen pizza dough pucks, and others asked for snacks like chips and crackers. Reflecting on that night, I learned another valuable lesson, which I will reflect on in a later chapter—that one of the mistakes we made as a business in our early days was not expanding as much as possible our relationship with our best customer, HEB grocery.

Fulfilling our first "real" order

With the $10,000 in hand, Matt and I went to work trying to figure out how we were going to actually supply the grocery stores we were told were coming our way. Now we were trying to figure out a co-packing situation that would allow us to get our order to HEB. We still had not met with the buyers after the pitch day to understand the final grocery count; all we knew was that we were going to be in stores at some point later that year. As we began trying to figure out options ranging from producing the product ourselves, contract manufacturing, or just licensing out the product itself and the brand, and just taking a part of the margin, our buyers for the baking aisle got back to us with a store count way higher than we had expected. As we were one of the winners of the cash prizes they really wanted to move forward with the momentum, so they wanted us to start in 168 stores with potential later that year to go up to 200 stores. For a company that only had volume at farmers markets and little distribution online, this was a huge step change for us.

Fulfilling this first order was absolutely wild. We had two months to essentially increase our production by an order of magnitude. Given that we were making the flour in-house, we started with that first. We hired our first employee, to work out of our facility and mill flour for us, as we searched for somebody to blend our breakfast mix. While this initial order was very high relative to where we had been for the last year, it was still very small volume for more traditional co-packers and co-manufacturers to take on. What started off as a seemingly easy search quickly became a very difficult hunt for somebody that could help quickly fulfill this order as time was starting to wind down for this first purchase order. At the same time, while this was going on, my investors got very excited about the prospect of this business actually taking off. I don't think I had ever seen them more positively involved during the last five years than at this moment. They were throwing out options for executive coaching and trying to use the momentum to raise money. I won't lie to you, this was one of the first of many emotional highs and exciting moments in the entrepreneurial journey that I was on. But, like with all highs, you have to come down eventually.

We were able to find a co-packer in Houston that would take on our limited volume. Although their reviews and general customer service from others who had used them were very poor, we figured we could work with them for one or two orders until we actually found somebody to help us build inventory later on. This was a mistake as we were very new still to the food industry, especially at a more commercial scale. Logistics, food safety, multi-point sourcing, packaging, you name it, we had not actually learned it yet. Because of the limited cash position we had, and the payment cycles from HEB from when we would deliver them our first order, we were limited to only making just enough for this order, which made a lot of our options on transportation very cost prohibitive, or so it seemed. I didn't really understand the value of my time as I was just mostly head down in the dirt trying to get the work done. Something I wish I had learned at that time early on.

I rented a sprinter van hauling all of the flour that would be used to make the pancake mix blends as well as the shipping supplies needed to deliver the products to the HEB warehouse. The folks in Houston were incredibly difficult to work with, giving us limited insight as to the progress of the product and how they were blending it. For food and really for any co-manufacturing agreement, this is a pretty hard pill to swallow, especially when the product is utilizing your brand and proprietary ingredients. You want to have oversight as to how the product is going without interfering too much in its actual development. While they were doing the blending in Houston for the pancake mix we were packaging the flour in San Antonio. Usually, in this scenario, once everything is done you call up a broker to find a truck for you that would then take the product and deliver it to the warehouse of your choosing. They would handle all the paperwork on-site and any appointments needed to make the delivery happen. But, because of my ignorance on this, we did all that ourselves.

We went out to Houston in a sprinter van, picked up all the finished products, brought that to San Antonio, and palletized everything including the finished flour that we had on-site, totaling eight pallets, when at the time the most that we'd ever done was half of one. I went out and rented a Penske truck, brought that over, and Matt and I loaded up all eight pallets into the truck. But because we did not have a forklift available to us, we had to un-palletize everything and re-palletize them in the truck. Mind you, it is at least 100 degrees Fahrenheit outside. I mentioned to you earlier that we were underfunded, but to give you just a brief idea and just how bad it was for us, in order to get access to a forklift I gave the lumberyard men Chick-fil-A once every three weeks in return for them driving over and handling a load or unload on call whenever needed. Now a lot of people like free food, but at some point the owners of the lumberyard got very pissed when they found this out. So in order to get a forklift, we found an auction where they were selling an electric forklift, from the 1990s, which we got for $2,200. There is a difference between being cheap and being frugal, and, unfortunately, we had to always side on the former.

Once we finally got the Penske truck loaded, I began driving out to the warehouse not knowing what paperwork I needed, or which loading dock to go to, just the address for where the purchase order said that this order needed to be delivered to. En route, because Matt and I did not know how to stack pallets in a truck, when I took a turn too sharply I could hear the thud of every pallet getting knocked down from the tilting of the truck. With great despair, I walked out of the truck after pulling off to the side of the road, opened the back, and saw hundreds of boxes all over the truck. I frantically called Matt, and he turned around while he was on his way home after helping load up the truck in the first place, and we spent the next two hours restacking all the boxes. Still to this day, I'm surprised an officer never pulled us over and talked to us about what we were doing. Because it was so hot you had two dudes, shirtless, loading up what looked like unmarked boxes in the back of a truck, only a few hours away from the border, and in a city that has had a lot of drug issues in the past. Once everything was reloaded, I drove out to the HEB warehouse, but because I did not have the paperwork I was forced to wait nearly five hours on the side of the road while the buyer helped confirm with the warehouse what our products were and what the reconciliation would need to be with the information at the warehouse. Once everything was loaded, swearing to myself I would never do this again, I drove home and slept for what felt like several days.

Shooting for the stars and almost landing on the moon

As they always say in business, it's not getting the customer that's the hard part, it's keeping them. Part of that with CPGs is that you need to play your part in increasing the volume to make sure the store, which already operates at a very thin margin, remains incentivized to keep you on board. When we first started at HEB in the fall of 2019, our volumes were incredibly low. Yet we were determined to make a change. With the help of several HEB programs, privy to only those that attended the Quest competition, we were able to utilize several promotions to help bolster the presence of our product in stores. We went through several demos in stores, coupons, partnering with in-store chefs at various HEB stores around the state, and anything and everything that could get the performance of our product up. Within three months of starting off at the stores we were able to improve our performance almost fourfold.

Additionally, there were several papers, podcasts, and other news coming out about us since winning the competition. Not only did we have citywide recognition in San Antonio, but state and nationwide recognition as well.

All of this got the attention of several investors, including HEB's venture arm. As we started realizing that we needed to raise money fast in order to just support our presence inside HEB, we had our eyes on a much larger prize, a significant seed round that would allow us to accelerate the growth of the business in stores as well as allow us the ability to begin exploring two new avenues of future growth: wholesale, and technology licensing. I began meeting with several angel and venture investors around the country, as well as accelerators, in addition to HEB's venture arm.

These meetings began to take shape and get traction in January 2020. After several meetings, and beginning the process of due diligence, we were able to get to a point where our agreed-upon valuation was just north of $5 million, post money, and more importantly, the prospects of this becoming a successful venture were really within grasp. As with all things, as I've learned running a business, everything takes longer than you anticipate. Unfortunately, the due diligence process began really taking form in March of 2020. I remember this day so vividly. We finished a meeting and pitch to several senior leaders at HEB and had some time in the hallway to chat a bit more candidly with them after the set time. Things in Asia and Europe were already escalating as the Covid pandemic began spreading. There was a lot of worry among the HEB leaders of supply chain concerns, although to their credit they had already been preparing for this pandemic since December when the first rumors of the disease were spreading in China, a region which HEB relies a lot on for many materials.

We were told by the folks we pitch to that we would hear back within a week about the next steps. But one week went by, and then another, and then another. One day, I get a text from a buddy showing me a post on social media that the NBA was canceled after a star player got Covid. That evening I got an email saying that HEB was tabling all discussions within their venture group for the time being as the focus completely shifted to managing the ensuing chaos for the next what would be two years.

We did not know what to expect from the business side, and although very disappointed that the investment round failed, we still had an operation to run. Might be hard for some people to remember, but there was mass dysphoria and fear running rampant as people did not know what to believe or what to think of the pandemic as it began to take shape in the United States. Mass hoarding at grocery stores of essential supplies which then quickly spread to nearly every item, including ours. All the inventory that we had planned for the next few months at HEB and online was then rerouted to all the grocery stores in order to support the nearly five times demand. We did not have a great cash position to be able to wait to get payment for those orders in order to then resupply the now emptied online presence and grocery store shelves. Even once we were able to get our products back on shelves, after about a month, the damage was already done. The lack of inventory and momentum that we had built in the fall was all but eviscerated overnight seemingly. To make matters worse, there was an enormous shift in ecommerce that heavily unfavored small businesses. As people were shifting to shopping online more and more, the cost to promote and advertise became increasingly expensive as auctioning and bidding for ad placement both on social media and other web-based platforms increased at some points by almost sixfold. This mixture led to what I described in Chapter 1 as a shit show. We lost everything and didn't see an order come through from HEB for nearly two months.

With increasing tension from the board, and myself, Matt used the time and opportunity to leave and pursue a new career; who could blame him. He had been married for a year, and was looking to begin the next chapter of his life. I too at this moment began looking for what to do next in my life, and had decided to pursue an MBA, thinking that my engineering and brief entrepreneurial journey would make one heck of a story to an admission board. But, as you know, the story did not end there. We got a second wind, and would try for another two and a half years to solve the problem of food waste at a commercial scale.

10

Growth, "failure", and what the future holds

How I led an effortful and diligent pivot, but ultimately could not succeed in bringing this business to the next stage—winter 2020 to present

After getting the grant from TechFuel and getting our loan forgiven from the city, other things began to seemingly fall into place. We began getting traction with the wholesale side of our business, with customers asking for samples and ordering small volumes of our upcycled flour directly from us. One of those key customers was HEB grocery. If you're familiar with a lot of grocery stores, you'll know that many of them have in-store bakeries. At a chef's discretion, they would work with local distributors to source these ingredients, bring them into stores partially baked or as fresh ingredients, prepare them, and sell them to customers at various locations around the state. HEB had noticed that there was a trend coming for more unique baked items, including upcycled ingredients, and through just a lot of the work that we had done within stores early on when we first got into their network, we were known as the upcycled go-to experts internally. This was actually a great learning experience for us, and led to some very key pivotal decisions for us.

First major learning was professionalizing our appearance to customers. A key thing within food is the food safety aspect, obviously. The real challenge with food safety is both the appearance of food safety as well as the actual policy, procedures, and execution. I don't think I worked harder over the subsequent years than when I was developing our food safety procedures on how we execute orders with quality and consistency, and establishing these programs to be executed not only by me, but also by our partners and employees.

Second learning was on the economics of evaluating long-term and long-tail risks with decisions. At this moment in our company history, we had established, while still nascent, a brand that provided CPG products on grocery store shelves and online. However, the economics of selling products in bulk were much more enticing to us. The resulting gross margins when selling our flour in 20- to 50-pound sacks were nearly three to four times larger than when we were selling products via store shelves. But the required volume to get profitable within the CPG side of the business was very high, while the volume required on the wholesale end of things seemed more achievable at that time. As we started to see some of these orders and inquiries come in, and began evaluating what this would look like financially, the strategy that we drummed up was that we would utilize the wholesale cash flow to fund the growth on the CPG side, which we believed would cause a virtuous cycle of educating the marketplace using our branded items leading to more wholesale orders, which yielded more cash, which would then help fund more CPG sales, and so on. While this strategy seemed great on paper, to execute it was a whole different story. In my estimation, with plenty of hindsight bias, I truly believe that this alongside Covid was the real domino that would inevitably cause the business to fail long term.

As we got more and more inquiries, we began to see that the capacity of our pilot plant would not be able to handle the wholesale volume that we were seeing. The equipment we had was being held together, no joke, by tape and rope. As we were bursting at the seams, we really had to make a choice whether or not to pursue the wholesale side, which would require a lot more capacity, a larger plant, and more financing. As a board, we decided that this investment was worth the risk, and began to pursue a financing round to help get us to a place where we could supply this seemingly growing wholesale base of potential customers. As we were searching for equity, and exploring a capital call with existing investors, a couple of things played out that helped get us a bit closer to what we needed.

Financing falling into place and building our first production-scale plant

First, we got a grant from the Kroger Co. Foundation, to help promote upcycling. This was structured as an accelerator with the first portion of the grant provided in the early spring of 2021, and the last portion provided at the end of the program toward December 2021. We began exploring the route of an SBA loan, to help fund the expansion of our process; however, there were several complications that did not give us the ability to do that. So we decided to take out a traditional business loan, using our own collateral, to be able to get another portion of the financing required. Lastly, we were able to execute a reinvestment from our existing shareholder base, leading us to raise almost $750,000 when you add up all the grants, loans, and equity. While we really needed twice that amount, we felt this would be enough to give us one year's worth of runway, and show and prove the technology at a larger commercial scale, execute some of these customer orders, and use that momentum to help bring in more money.

As the end of 2020 and the beginning of 2021 progressed, we found our lease, began the accelerator, and started the process of moving to the new facility and purchasing the new equipment. Unfortunately, Covid reared its ugly head again. You might remember there was a computer chip shortage for new cars due to many factories shutting down, leading to a large undersupply in the market. Well, our equipment ran on some of those computer chips, leading to nearly three to four months of delays for the new plant. So, while we thought by early summer we would have an operating facility, it wasn't until September that we would have our first production run at the new plant.

To use that time, I worked on developing partnerships with new suppliers, marketing our potential new capacity, trying to bring in new customers, and educating customers and the community at large about what upcycling was and what our mission as a business revolved around. This included events at SXSW, various forms of local engagement, and networking with other businesses in Texas, the United States, and abroad.

It's now the fall of 2021, we have our equipment finally installed, about four to five months left of our runway, and a few customers in the hopper. As I mentioned before, we made the decision to build the facility and pursue a business in wholesale supply. Now, in order to do this, and later secure funding, the new facility and subsequent processes and business model need to answer two critical questions for the space of upcycling.

Question one, can this be done at scale? This revolved around the questions of supply and production. Supply needed to be food-safe, consistent, and procured profitably. The second question is, will people buy it?

Well, the second question was answered pretty quickly. as we got our first large contract with HEB bakery earlier that year in 2021, leading to the decision to make the bet on wholesale. However, this is a huge learning experience on both real sale cycles, and the effect of relying on others for marketing decisions. HEB decided to go the route of promoting the product as a "beer bread". No joke, this bread had even more carbs than your regular loaf of bread. The issue with this route was that it did not promote either of the two benefits when going with the product that we were providing. Our flour was low carb, high protein, high fiber, and most importantly, upcycled, meaning it was great for the environment. None of those things were promoted, and I also did not push to promote those things when in initial discussions with their baking team. I was relying on them to make the best decisions for us, when in reality they had limited data, and were making the best decisions for them. No one to blame but myself.

So, when a local business, C. H. Guenther, which is a powerhouse international bakery headquartered in San Antonio, contacted us for a new initiative to supply United States Foods, I wanted to make sure they utilized our learnings from the market in the last three and a half years. They were exploring upcycling and wanted to start with a burger bun. We already had some other customers and learned quickly to jump alongside them early on. We knew the sales cycle for wholesale ingredients was choppy at best, so the best chance for success was that we really needed to be the best partner both in development, helping market and sell their final product, and being a great ingredient supplier when the time came.

The launch of the first commercial product made with our ingredients and attempting to scale

We absolutely needed this product to take off as we were running out of money. But, as luck would have it, when the product was in development, I was unable to make my suggestions heard. They decided to go with a burger bun dubbed the "pub grain bun", very similar to the HEB bread that ended up nearly flopping in all the markets that it launched in. Even though the product did not necessarily follow what I had wished, the initial order was substantial. Far more than my one employee could handle. We originally decided to hire staff for our operation, starting with a supervisor, and working our way to production folks. We did a couple trial runs for the first three weeks and then began full-swing production toward the end of November of 2021. At this point, I was pretty burnt out and took a couple weeks to head back to Colorado in order to recuperate and get the ball rolling on the order when I got back in January. In the meantime, the staff would work in lieu of me, start on the production, and then head home for the holidays, with the expectation that we would hit the gas pedal when we all returned after New Year.

When we got back and started production we had two and a half months left of runway, so our board was aware that a capital call was coming in order to fulfill this order, and subsequent orders, and using that as the proof of concept, needed to begin a fundraise that would adequately capitalize the business. Like our pilot plant, the equipment that we were able to afford for the new facility was not by any means state-of-the-art except for the patented piece of technology that was our dryer. For the next month, I would end up spending close to 40 hours at the facility just in production alone, on top of everything else that we had going on. I was trying to hire anybody with a pulse to help us fulfill this order so that we could at least get this first large batch out the door. By the end of January we finally had it done, with many hiccups and things breaking along the way, and I remember the feeling of seeing a semi-truck full of our flour heading out to a bakery to be baked into bread. It was incredibly rewarding, but frightening as I realized this scenario would keep happening again and again, until something changed.

Once we were able to get the capital call done with our board, extending our runway to the end of fall, I decided that my time was best spent trying to market the business with some of the data that we had from this last order, and raise a seed round. So, in order to do this, I needed to hire some more staff at the facility in order to manage the day-to-day operations, so that I could focus on raising money. The issue with this was that I failed to transfer the learnings of operating the equipment from earlier in the year in a clean and sustainable way to my supervisor and production operators. Additionally, I failed to establish a routine of gathering clean data from the facility, in order to really understand how things were operating. While I was in a better habit of communicating with the board than in the previous year, just the business of the operation, and the fact that I was essentially doing all this on my own, led me to severely drop the ball on communicating with the board on a regular interval on our financials, production and operations updates, and just the overall state of the business. This eventually led to an effect where I was operating in a black box, not receiving much help from the board. Albeit, I should have drawn the line and essentially demanded that we go and get the resources required to make the business work, or that we just stop operating altogether, save some money, and just shut things down otherwise. This is a level of confidence and clarity that I lacked at the time. So I kept operating in the way that we did, trying to not only sell more product, but also find potential investors, as well as keeping the operational afloat. 2022 was a year marked with many cycles of burnout, of me not really getting anywhere, as I was trying to go everywhere at once. To make matters worse, the facility had begun to not operate nearly as well as it had earlier in the year, with production efficiency as well as our food safety standards beginning to drop steadily throughout the year.

One final attempt to pivot

This culminated into an enormous blow-up when we received our largest order to date, from a competitor looking to private label and co-manufacture our process and product for their customers. What the space of upcycling began to realize was that, in general, it was very unprofitable to operate upcycling when approached like a traditional food business. In reality what we began to realize as an industry was that certain products would require more education for customers to get on board, while others, for example upcycled fruit, did not require a lot of education for customers, who easily adapted their purchasing decisions to make the leap to buy some of those products. Additionally, profitability was hard to come by, as maintaining a high level of food safety and production efficiency without adequate upfront investment was nearly impossible.

I began to realize that the only route forward for this business was for the technology to be installed in a co-located fashion next to a food and beverage manufacturer where their byproducts and refuse would be collected on-site and upcycled on-site into a shelf-stable product. The current design of operating a centrally located facility was highly uneconomic until you reached scales that we would not get to anytime soon. The ask for the fundraise began to evolve, as these learnings became clearer throughout the year. I began looking for a financer and or a food and beverage manufacturer to pilot and fund our technology at their location. The economies of scale were incredibly appealing. As this pivot became clearer to me, I communicated with our board that this was probably the route we should go, and they agreed. We started looking for a potential partner in a very large brewery or beverage manufacturer and even conducted pilots with some incredibly notable names. We expanded the application of our technology to show use cases ranging from oat pulp to fruit pomace, coffee grounds, and refuse from bread manufacturing. We worked with our legal advisors to expand the intellectual property, and I worked closely with my past and current mentors to formulate a package that would be presented to these potential partners. The ask was relatively straightforward: license or buy our technology, and we will help you upcycle on-site at a scale that will allow us to reach a price point that will get more people through the door, and we will help sell the product, whether through a co-branded CPG item utilizing their highly recognized brands, or as just an ingredient to be utilized by others.

And we were starting to see some interesting conversations take form, but the focus was just not there as the operation was still in place and required attention from me. Once the order came in, it became clear that I had been incredibly negligent of our facility operations, and had been too focused on what would later be deemed as "distractions". While I believe those "distractions" were important to evaluate when you are working alone, the most valuable asset you have is time, and unfortunately I was spending my time on things that did not bring in much-needed revenue for a business that was nearing the end of its runway.

While I had been pressuring our board to fundraise with the momentum we had at the end of 2021 and the beginning of 2022, the early investors were very concerned with dilution. For many, when fundraising, it is difficult to get money in the first place. However, when working with existing shareholders, usually with the first right of refusal, this is a common issue. There is a worry about dilution as they are looking to retain or grow their proportion of ownership. When working with venture capital firms or experienced venture investors, the same is felt, but to a much lesser degree. The understanding is clear that, in order for the question or pressures of being diluted to mean anything, there has to be a sizeable pie in the first place. It is very difficult to bring in new sources of funding when the cap table is "messy" and there are outsized owners. This was the case, and presented problems when presenting the business to potential investors. Additionally, because of the worry on dilution, as a board, there will be pressure to ask for less than what's needed, on the overestimation of the ability to use the lesser funds and achieve similar outcomes to what would have been done with more funding. While I agree that more money is not the answer (most times), in our case, there was such a severe lack of funding, we were essentially always betting that a customer would come through and provide the required funding through income to propel the business forward. I had seen this clearly and wanted to mitigate that as funding for early-stage startups was still more available earlier on in the year. But those requests were never met, and I was forced to chart my own path. However, in glorious fashion, we were unable to succeed in supplying the competitor that approached us. Combined with my lack of focus at the facility and a lack of planning out the production, we were unable to support the customer's order and failed to deliver. This led to the board stepping in and deciding that I was out as CEO.

At this point, we had worked our way through the runway as I predicted, and were stuck with a decision: do we continue or call it quits? Our board director at the time and a leading investor decided to give it one last go, and with the votes from the board members approving the motion, they added more capital in to see if there was a chance to not only recoup our customers, but also grow to a steady state of production and increased sales over the next six months in order to find a viable partner or buyer for the business. So my focus transitioned from doing CEO duties to focusing on looking for viable investors, partners, or anyone that could help finance the potential that we sought. After a few months of trying to stabilize the business, satisfy customers' purchase orders, and search for potential investors, it became clear to us that this business would not have a viable future at this rate, and the decision was made to effectively shut down the business while looking for strategic options for future licensing of our technology. And that was the abrupt conclusion of Grain4Grain. While the complete end would take a bit longer, the operation effectively shut down and we were no longer creating new product or actively participating in the market. Once all the inventory had been sold, we closed our doors and moved to looking for a strategic exit by finding a home for the technology, processes, and knowledge we built in the space.

I have made plenty of mistakes in this venture. While some were glaringly obvious at the time, many were more apparent once the day-to-day emotions settled in and I was able to perform almost a postmortem. Here are some thoughts during this process as this is still relatively fresh as of writing this book.

Lessons learned on partnerships and investors

When creating a venture there are so many people or stakeholders involved that it may not seem so obvious when starting. When starting Grain4Grain the first people involved were the founders and initial investors. My perspective in the beginning, which I still hold today, is that you don't necessarily need a co-founder, but you do need somebody, with some level of authority, that balances out the lacking skill sets of the primary driver for any organization or project. This could be a CEO who reports to a partner that's less involved but has enough skin in the game where there are aligned incentives for the business to succeed. This could be a founder whose first employee carries some equity but balances out the personalities and skill sets carried by the CEO. There are tons of examples where you don't necessarily need co-founders starting with equal stake in the business. For our situation, there were some clear red flags in our approach to creating our equity distribution. Matt and I both, early on, agreed to have me be the first full-time person while Matt would cover my living expenses and still maintain a full-time job. While this worked out well in the early days, as we didn't necessarily need two full-time people, Matt got to keep his job, and I didn't need to milk my savings—the opportunity cost in hindsight of what we forewent when we had only one full-time person was far too high and I believe greatly outweighed the early benefits.

For example, in the early days, you have absolutely no idea what you are actually doing beyond some level of clarity on the product you are offering and some of those early potential customers. The job of the founders is to find early adopters that are going to pay real money for your product and try to learn as fast as possible exactly what they are using it for and what they are not using it for, and apply those learnings quickly and efficiently. Our product was a CPG and required many people to make a sizable revenue stream when consuming our products. Additionally, in the early days, we did aspire to our technology one day being utilized by people and a wholesale business, but this would have been a distraction for just one person to do full time. But with two people, there may have been some discoveries and or more data collected on the actual performance of our equipment and the potential uptake of wholesale products in the marketplace.

All of these hypothetical situations, while made up, present the real challenges in the early days of a venture that absolutely require focus for answering and solving those problems. Another mistake we made was our investor base was not venture oriented, but rather mostly experienced in private equity. While the discipline that they pushed was absolutely necessary, and frankly advice I should have listened to more, the risk profile was very different to what they were used to. This made board meetings, strategy sessions, fundraising efforts, and operational focus often very misaligned. In hindsight, I wish that the board, and I believe that wish is also based on other founders' experiences, had been more involved in a way of providing more guidance in the early technology phase and operations of Grain4Grain. The board we ended up assembling was far more appropriate for more mature businesses.

Lessons learned on finding your lane as an early-stage venture

Many authors have written about finding what makes you uniquely gifted as a business, whether it's the type of product you're offering or the customers that you have that are really great. In our instance this partner was HEB. HEB took us on in the early days, worked with us with the limited resources we had, and routinely tried to find ways to make us more successful, as our success would lead to their success. Rarely will you find a customer like that as one of your first customers. Unfortunately for us, the decision we made was to focus on things outside of that channel. What we failed to realize was that HEB was being an early adopter of our products, giving us an avenue for early growth as a business through utilizing our CPG line of business. While our CPG business did not have great margins and was severely damaged by Covid policies during the pandemic, HEB had still stuck around and was still vying for our success.

And, sure, while we did have new opportunities presenting themselves within wholesale and some potential utilizations of our technology, we had a great customer that we did not do our absolute best to serve. While again I'm benefiting from hindsight bias, there might have been opportunities for us to recover our business in grocery stores, get new products on the shelves, and do everything within our power to make those products fly off those shelves. When you have a great customer, take care of them, and fire any other customer or line of work that's distracting you from providing the absolute best service and product to your best customer. Obviously this changes as you grow and are looking for new lines of revenue, but as a startup, do not be distracted from that singular focus of finding a great customer and taking care of that great customer, period. Always take care of the hand that feeds you. You don't have much time or runway to do otherwise—even if you raise millions. Focus all your time and energy into delighting that customer, learning everything you can from them, and letting them guide you to the next phase of growth when the time comes. Neglecting our best early customer was a pivotal mistake, and one I hope to never repeat in the future.

Lessons learned on the partners and people we worked with

Lastly, because of the lack of clear direction and vision that I needed to and should have provided, the people, partners, and employees we brought on became burdensome rather than helpful in many ways. What I mean by burdensome is that, without clear direction, almost all contributions and efforts made by all those around tend to provide more obstacles to the organization than wins. When looking to figure out what our business should be doing, had we focused on say just CPG, or just wholesale, or just our technology, we likely would have been able to steadily accomplish what we set out to do, rather than a shotgun approach. Now, there is something to be said when you have a board that is asking about EBITDA and dividends for an early-stage business—but at the end of the day, when wearing the CEO hat, the reins ultimately fall on you (and me in this case) to provide the direction and clarity needed for success. In the same breath, the CEO also becomes a burden without this vision and focus. It is so easy to become overextended, it feels like it can happen virtually overnight. When there is not a clear sense of vision coming from the top, everybody, including the CEO, becomes overextended and directionless. Without a solid foundation of what we had as a business, it was only a matter of time for us to run out of resources, overextend our people and partners, and ultimately fail to deliver on what we set out to do.

We had several successes with people. Matt and I balanced each other out with personalities, and just how we operated in an uncertain environment. Matt is heavily analytical and is able to analyze the situations and the various potential outcomes very well. I am very resourceful, generally good with people, and I'm also able to understand complex topics and apply those learnings quickly. This allowed for me and Matt to think through some of the difficult situations that the business presented us in a way that played to our strengths and limited our weaknesses, as best we could.

We were able to find phenomenal partners and early employees that were pivotal to the progress we made. I already mentioned HEB as being one of those partners, but this extends to mentors, strategic suppliers, and other folks that helped us along the way. It goes a long way presenting yourself as a likable person, and Matt and I were able to really, just through being kind and generous with our time and knowledge, get and achieve a lot in the early days. I remember we had an employee volunteer to stay many hours past his scheduled shift, to make sure our first order made it out the door. I saw breweries that we worked with really step up when they were getting nothing when we were piloting with them. We were able to get so much exposure through just the mentors that I was able to work with and get advice from, and learned an immense amount of business both in food and just general business operations throughout the years.

Building a strong team and support network was pivotal in getting as far as we did. I'm grateful to this day for the talented people who joined us on the journey and gave it their all. Their efforts taught me that success is never achieved alone. Surround yourself with people who share your values and complement your abilities. Compensate them fairly, treat them with respect, and make sure to express your appreciation. The relationships you build through startup ups and downs can be some of the most meaningful.

Lessons learned from mismanaged finances and failed strategy at Grain4Grain

The ultimate killer of most businesses is failed finances. For us in particular, and for most startups that are equipment and "top" heavy to get going, the front-end capital expenditures are generally very high and require proper investment. Now, this does not mean you have to spend a whole lot of money to get things going, but there is a very big difference between being frugal versus being cheap. When you have limited resources to begin with, the temptation is to be cheap. But as I mentioned earlier, when there is clear focus, you can drive frugality in the business in the early days and really throughout the business's life. But when you are cheap, like we were in many ways, it tends to come back to bite you if you have any reasonable amount of success reaching customers and achieving sales. Your ability to deliver becomes sandbagged and limited to the investment you've made in your equipment. Being frugal says you don't need to have the extra things to make things easier. Being cheap says you will forego the adequate amount of investment, and or take shortcuts with the type of equipment you get to try and achieve said objective.

It was very clear in the early days that we did not have the investment required to adequately deliver to customers at the scale that we were hoping to achieve. When that realization was made, we should have gathered the learnings we had, and looked for an investor, or partner, to bring things up to par to continue delivering or our vision. Additionally, we made poor assessments of the various market signals we were getting. While we did not have a lot of data as we had very limited touch points and the market was very nascent, we did have some glimpses as to what the market was saying to our other partners and competitors in the space of upcycled products. We knew this space lacked a lot of pricing power as it was positioned within the ingredients space, which was already impacted by decades of efficiencies in America, leading us to have almost no pricing power when trying to sell to large customers. When we decided to bring our price down in the hopes of achieving adequate volumes to suffice that hamstrung margin, we already signed our death wish as we were now trying to compete with some of the most efficient food manufacturers in the country.

This leads me back to my earlier points of deciding between CPG and wholesale. CPG channels offer more flexibility and control with pricing as you are able to target certain customer groups, and are not reliant on your end customer, as you would be with wholesale, to adequately reach that customer. We were selling something that in the early days was meant for people with slightly higher income, but our wholesale customers were selling things that were not properly priced to customers that were not making those higher income ranges. This can lead to many issues including declining free cash flows, which indicates and signals some of these problems, and less control on revenue sources leading to what we experienced of batchy orders and long sale cycles. The market was also telling us that this space was in many ways mostly smoke and mirrors. Meaning that corporate pressures for ESG concerns were generally met with greenwashed efforts for sustainability. One of the signals was that, while the barrier to entry was low, very few people were receiving large investments, signaling that this space was largely operated by organizations that did not have a ton of revenue but were getting a lot of attention as the potential was allegedly there. This indicated that most companies really did not actually care a ton about upcycling and would become late adopters in the space after several brands in the CPG realm created enough awareness and demand for upcycled goods. While this is a generalization, it matches conventional wisdom that your early adopters are generally the small mom-and-pop bakeries, individual customers, and other smaller outlets instead of your big and major corporations.

Rather than me going around and knocking on every single small bakery in Texas, I focused my energy and attention on big customers, which would move the needle to success with just them providing repeat orders. If I could do it all over again, I would just focus all my attention on HEB, achieve success there, and then focus on growing our uptake of our ingredients locally, then statewide, then look toward national customers, in that order. There are obviously many other mistakes financially that we made, but these are the principal and fundamental ones.

Parting thoughts

All these failures and successes were a rough education, but I am fortunate in many ways. I did not necessarily lose my shirt, so there might be another try for me in the future. I've had the opportunity to apply some of these learnings to my family's business, in terms of organizing and professionalizing some of the services they offer. Additionally, I have been looking to expand some of their offerings in order to strategically serve their customers better. I plan to go work full time somewhere, in order to also apply these learnings while developing some of the skills that I lack. So yes, I am going to consider this as a five-year, very rough, MBA, in which I was able to really learn how to do something in the real world. Very few things in life are as satisfying as getting a paying customer for something you spent so long and hard thinking on and working at.

To conclude I will leave some encouragement based on the learnings that I've had, largely to encourage myself, but also any reader that is looking to be an entrepreneur or develop something on their own, whether within an organization or just a project.

One, respect cash flow. Whether you are running a high-powered startup, building a small business, running a side hustle, or whatever it is, in this world cash is your life's blood. Without it, things begin to atrophy, be undernourished, and, heaven forbid, die. Have a fundamental understanding of where you are at, where your money is coming from, where your money is going, and, most importantly, who you owe, whether that is a lender or the government, in the form of taxes; always know where you stand. If properly done, within 20 seconds you should be able to know if you are in trouble, successful, or maybe even underinvesting in your business or project. There are hundreds if not thousands of resources out there to help you understand the premise of cash flow, and there is no excuse to not have that understanding, especially after reading that book. Now, if you don't have a knack for that, or maybe just the time, bring in somebody, who carries authority, to help see and understand your finances. Don't get distracted by all of those newsletters and PR releases of huge fundraisers from companies and startups; the money will come when you practice stern discipline on your finances. There are many reasons why you may not have profitability, but having a stern grip on where you are at and where you are going with your cash flow, even if it's negative, will allow you to get that financing, especially when things are tough.

Two, expect the worst and prepare for the best. While this euphemism is widely said and generally understood, my approach and perspective expands on this a bit more. When expecting for the worst and preparing for the best, you are expecting in the future that there are going to be highly difficult periods where any inefficiencies that exist will poison the organization from the inside out. This could be the wrong people, not practicing healthy redundancies like preventing rework through the common practice of measuring twice but building once, or not having clear systems in place, regardless of how simple or small they may be. When engineers are able to figure out the business, they tend to make great entrepreneurs because they're able to think systematically about their practices and are able to think through scaling and organization as they would scale a mechanical piece of equipment or digital process. So, if you do not have that experience thinking through systems as engineers do, it's wise to find resources that help you understand the systems of your organization, the things that need to be done, and how to prioritize them and delegate those tasks. However, engineers can also complicate things naturally so understanding the fine line between unnecessary redundancies and healthy processes is a practice that eludes even the best leaders. So, keeping this top of mind all the time, regardless of how big or small you are, will be paramount to your future success.

Three, advisors. I already mentioned this earlier; you do not necessarily need a co-founder, but you do need an advisor. Whether it's a board of advisors that retain an unofficial role in the organization or a board of directors, you need somebody that will hold you accountable, so that you can also effectively hold others accountable. Practicing clear and concise communication, whether that's monthly reports, quarterly reports, basic financial reports, and other forms of communication, is a very important practice that will help you in more ways than you'll realize. This type of high-level review always gets the entrepreneur out of the weeds and helps bring in clarity, for whatever the task at hand or goals are.

Four, listen. I know I don't have to repeat why listening is more important than talking, but I can't even begin to emphasize that it is as important for an organization as it is for the individual and leader. Listening means listening to your customers, listening to the market, listening to your employees, and listening to your partners. For so many, including us, you fall into the fallacy of building a product thinking you know the market, or the environment in which you're practicing, and begin trying to push this thing into the hands of customers when they are really asking for something else. The humility of being able to listen and adapt to the needs of the people you are serving is what will distinguish you from everyone else. But more importantly, listening allows you to get more data, while it might be biased, allows you to minimize room for luck and randomness, and allows for skill to grow. There's a quote by Alexis Carrel that I like: "A few observations and much reasoning lead to error; many observations and a little reasoning to truth". The premise is simple: the more you listen, the more you learn; and the more you learn, the more probable it is that you will be better positioned for success and ultimately give your customers a service that they will not only come back to but also bring others to.

Thank you so much for taking the time to read this. If you made it this far I am immensely grateful to you for reading this story of me and my family. While I wish I was writing this in better circumstances, with more of an open end had we been more successful in achieving our goals with Grain4Grain, I think there will be a second act sometime in the future. I wish all who read this plenty of success, however you define that, and implore you to reach out if you ever want to talk about what you're working on or what I'm working on. Good luck and Godspeed.

Notes

1. For more information on the various global revolutions and their impact on world history, I recommend the following books: *Revolution and Rebellion in the Early Modern World* by Jack A. Goldstone; *Revolutionary Movements in World History: From 1750 to the Present* by James DeFronzo; and *World Order* by Henry Kissinger.

2. For more readings on the USSR's technological programs and advancements, the books I recommend are: *Red Plenty* by Francis Spufford; *Engineering Communism: How Two Americans Spied for Stalin and Founded the Soviet Silicon Valley* by Steven T. Usdin; and *Sputnik: The Shock of the Century* by Paul Dickson.

3. For more information on the subject of effectuation, read *Causation and Effectuation: Toward a Theoretical Shift from Economic Inevitability to Entrepreneurial Contingency* by Saras Sarasvathy.

Suggested questions and assignments

Questions

1. What were the key mistakes Yoni made in the early stages of starting Grain4Grain? How could these have been avoided?

2. How did Yoni's immigrant background shape his entrepreneurial journey? In what ways did it help or hinder him?

3. Evaluate Yoni's decision to expand into wholesale ingredients instead of focusing solely on the CPG business. What factors should be weighed in strategic expansion decisions?

4. Discuss the role that financing played in the trajectory of Grain4Grain. How could Yoni have made better financial decisions?

5. Analyze Yoni's board of directors. What could he have done differently in assembling and working with the board?

6. Assess Yoni's relationship with anchor customer HEB. What lessons can be learned about nurturing key early adopter partnerships?

7. How did the Covid-19 pandemic impact Grain4Grain's operations and viability? What contingencies could small businesses undertake to withstand external shocks?

8. Discuss the challenges of scaling sustainable production technologies like upcycling. How can the "proof of concept" hurdles be overcome?

9. What leadership qualities did Yoni exhibit throughout his entrepreneurial journey? Which areas could he improve upon?

10. Imagine you are an investor considering Grain4Grain today. What advice would you give Yoni moving forward? Would you invest in a future venture of his?

Assignments

1. Develop a business and perform a "pre-mortem" by analyzing the various ways the business could fail. Some themes to follow are financial stresses, challenges with partnerships, and market-related obstacles.

2. If you could start a business tackling upcycling, what would you do? How would you navigate the early challenges to help increase the chances of success for your upcycling business?

Reference

Sarasvathy, S. D. (2001). Causation and effectuation: Toward a theoretical shift from economic inevitability to entrepreneurial contingency. *Academy of Management Review*, 26(2), 243–263.

Recommended further reading

DeFronzo, J. (2006). *Revolutionary Movements in World History: From 1750 to the Present*. Santa Barbara, CA: ABC-CLIO.

Dickinson, P. (2019). *Sputnik: The Shock of the Century*. Nebraska: University of Nebraska Press.

Goldstone, J. A. (2016). *Revolution and Rebellion in the Early Modern World: Population Change and State Breakdown in England, France, Turkey, and China, 1600–1350*. New York: Routledge.

Kissinger, H. (2015). *World Order: Reflections on the Character of Nations and the Course of History*. London: Penguin Books.

Sarasvathy, S. (2001). Causation and effectuation: Toward a theoretical shift from economic inevitability to entrepreneurial contingency. *Academy of Management Review*, 26(2), 243–263.

Spufford, F. (2011). *Red Plenty*. London: Faber & Faber.

Usdin, S. T. (2005). *Engineering Communism: How Two Americans Spied for Stalin and Founded the Soviet Silicon Valley*. Yale: Yale University Press.

Index